P9-ELG-974

MORE ALIKE
THAN DIFFERENT

My Life with Down Syndrome

DAVID EGAN
WITH KATHLEEN EGAN

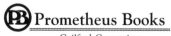
Prometheus Books

Guilford, Connecticut

PB Prometheus Books

An imprint of The Rowman & Littlefield Publishing Group, Inc.
4501 Forbes Blvd., Ste. 200
Lanham, MD 20706
www.rowman.com

Distributed by NATIONAL BOOK NETWORK

Copyright © 2020 by David Egan

All rights reserved. No part of this book may be reproduced in any form or
by any electronic or mechanical means, including information storage and
retrieval systems, without written permission from the publisher, except by
a reviewer who may quote passages in a review.

British Library Cataloguing in Publication Information Available

Library of Congress Cataloging-in-Publication Data

Names: Egan, David, 1977– author.
Title: More alike than different : my life with down syndrome / David Egan.
Description: Lanham, MD : Prometheus Books, 2020. | Summary: "In this
    inspiring memoir, David Egan tells his own story, authentically describing a
    life of maximizing his abilities, as he advocates for himself and for all other
    people with disabilities. This book is yet another first in a life that has seen
    many firsts, a life buoyed by an optimistic perspective that refuses to be limited
    by stereotypes and the low expectations of others."—Provided by publisher.
Identifiers: LCCN 2019057361 (print) | LCCN 2019057362 (ebook) | ISBN
    9781633886285 (cloth) | ISBN 9781633886292 (epub)
Subjects: LCSH: Egan, David, 1977– | Down syndrome—Patients—United
    States—Biography.
Classification: LCC RC571.E43 A3 2020 (print) | LCC RC571.E43 (ebook) |
    DDC 616.85/8842—dc23
LC record available at https://lccn.loc.gov/2019057361
LC ebook record available at https://lccn.loc.gov/2019057362

∞™ The paper used in this publication meets the minimum requirements of
American National Standard for Information Sciences—Permanence of Paper
for Printed Library Materials, ANSI/NISO Z39.48-1992.

CONTENTS

INTRODUCTION
The Myth of Limits

> David Egan has enriched my life in many important ways. He is a wonderful friend and mentor, and he has leadership skills that I can only hope to emulate. David inspires my work as a certified leadership coach. Whether my clients are C-suite executives or emerging organizational leaders, they benefit from the perspectives I have gained from observing David's emotional intelligence, authenticity, and executive presence. He's a man who defies limitations and eschews pretense. Imagine the potential of a nation with leaders like that.
>
> —Vince Randazzo, leadership coach[1]

I danced on my fortieth birthday at a big party, surrounded by friends and family.

That may not sound like much of an achievement to you, but there was more to celebrate than you can imagine.

And to be honest, at the time, it was just a big, fabulous party with music. There were lots of happy guests. People told me jokes about turning forty. All very ordinary stuff, but in a way, extraordinary.

On the day I was born in 1977, forty was well past the average age when people with Down syndrome died. Back then, the average lifespan for us was twenty-five. Having family and friends nearby was uncommon for people with Down syndrome. That's because so many of us lived in state-run institutions where people with intellectual disabilities were kept out of sight.

On the day I was born, it would have been almost impossible to believe that someone like me, someone with Down syndrome, could have gone through public schools and graduated as I did. To compete for a paid job and get it. To actively and confidently speak out in private and public on behalf of people with intellectual disabilities. To be the face of an international organization's advocacy in places throughout the world. To simply be out and about in the community, living my life alongside everyone else.

Those things that seemed impossible to the average person on the day I was born are commonplace today. And there is a simple reason why. It's because society started looking at people with disabilities as individuals.

In the 1970s, doctors, scientists, teachers, social workers, politicians, and, well, most everyone else thought that people with intellectual disabilities were all kind of the same. They figured that one person with Down syndrome was pretty much like every other person with Down syndrome. They saw limited potential, so they had no second thoughts about discarding us into institutions. Some families didn't do that, but most did because that's what doctors advised them to do.

The truth is that people with Down syndrome have a wide and wonderful range of abilities. Each person in the world has their own individual strengths, interests, skills, and weaknesses. The same is true for people with Down syndrome, of course. When passionate advocates began to fight for the right for each person to be seen as an individual, laws changed, and we began to prove ourselves in ways that are still surprising the world.

We have come so far since the bright, cool, sunny day in 1977, when my parents thought the world was crashing down around them because their first baby was born with Down syndrome. Down syndrome causes intellectual disability, they were told. It was hard news to hear for two young people working toward PhDs.

But here's where my story really begins. Mom and Dad didn't see me as a statistic or an example of a disability. They saw me as their baby, the sum of their traits, their own firstborn child. To them, I was David, their little David, and they loved me already. And they were used to making their own decisions.

An Audience of More Than Sixty Thousand

No matter the size of the audience, I always want to captivate them.

I always remember the words of Tim Shriver, my friend and chairman of Special Olympics: "If you touch one person's heart, it is worth your time."

That is good advice. I want to touch as many hearts as I can. In 2015, I stood in front of sixty thousand people in the Los Angeles Memorial Coliseum at the Special Olympics World Summer Games. I was also being broadcast throughout the world on TV.

That was the biggest audience I've ever spoken to directly. So far.

They worried, of course. Everything they were told had to do with limits and problems. They had no idea that society was already slowly changing.

They had no idea that one day their crying little David under lamps in the ICU would be the keynote speaker at the first National Down Syndrome Society (NDSS) adult summit in Washington, DC.

THE KEYNOTE SPEAKER

Fast forward thirty-plus years, and there I was, on that stage.

"Hello, everyone," I said to the big crowd in Washington, DC. "I am happy to see we are addressing issues that were not on past conference agendas."

My topic that day was about aging and how getting older affects people with Down syndrome. It's the kind of topic that people didn't talk about in the 1970s because our lifespan was so short. No one knew what to expect because so few people with Down syndrome lived past their forties.

One thing you need to know is, I talk in front of big crowds a lot. I'm always a little nervous and excited. I have a strong motivation to tell my story because I know it can make a difference when I do it. The audience that day was diverse. There were adults like me who had Down syndrome and their family members. But there were also caregivers, medical doctors, researchers, aging specialists, employers, educators, attorneys, financial advisors, and policy makers. It was an impressive group of people, and I had an important message to share.

Most of the people in the audience saw those of us with Down syndrome as individuals who had a diagnosis in common but not much else. And NDSS is a welcoming group that employs people with Down syndrome in key advocacy roles.

I was accepted as a leader and speaker without question or hesitation. Having Down syndrome was a plus because it gave me a point of view that mattered.

I want the entire world to see me that way. I'm a person you can describe in many different ways. Having Down syndrome is part of who I am, and it lets me see things in a way that other people can't. So in some ways it's important, but it's not the most important thing.

I grew up with parents who believed in developing and strengthening my abilities and not dwelling on my disability. They knew there is more to every human being than what you see at first glance.

WE ARE ALL COMPLEX PEOPLE

Most people are described by what they do well—an accomplished actor, a reliable mechanic, a knowledgeable accountant. Not many people are defined simply by a label or test score, but people with Down syndrome and other disabilities often are. That way of thinking puts us in a box with a label. That is too simple and neat to credit us with being the complex individuals we actually are.

Much of what people believe about those who are different from them are myths. If you believe a myth, you believe something that is not true. And if you base your behavior and attitudes on what is not true, then you may treat other people unfairly. Assumptions and fears of the unknown can put people you don't understand into uncomplicated boxes in your mind. If many people base their actions on myths or ignorance, the boxes become limits within society. And so many times, our own doubts can be made worse by the way others treat us. Doubts about yourself can keep you from seeing who you really are and who you can be.

That's why I am writing this book. I want to show that a big group of people who society underestimated and misunderstood has blossomed in thousands of ways as laws and attitudes changed. Compassionate, farsighted people have taken actions that changed the way people in the United States view people with disabilities, but there's more that needs to be done. I want to show that the potential of people with Down syndrome and other disabilities

> ### I Have Had Help with the Writing
>
> I know that you probably have never read a book written by someone with Down syndrome. Am I getting help? Sure I am. My mother and friends are helping me along the way. But that's not any different than most writers. Many people use editors and even ghostwriters to help tell their story. I'm not different. Well, that's not really true, of course. I am different. Just like you are.

grows as expectations grow. And expectations grow when there are examples of people who break barriers and do surprising things. They prove that limits are just another kind of myth. I have done all those things, as you will see.

Much of my life has been about finding limits within myself and going past them. That happened in sports, employment, education, and advocacy work. So I know my own expectations can both limit me and empower me.

At some point, each of us needs to speak up and act for ourselves. It's part of growing up, when a child gradually stops depending on parents for things and begins to make things happen on their own. That same process holds true for people with Down syndrome and other intellectual disabilities. People with disabilities are sometimes called self-advocates. It takes courage and belief in yourself to advocate for yourself. And when you do that, you can take the next step and speak up for others. That's a different kind of advocacy, and it's something I do a lot of, as you will see.

I mentioned boxes before. One of the boxes society has created is about being "smart." If a person has Down syndrome, developmental delays, autism, dyslexia, attention deficit disorder, or another condition that affects the outcomes of standard intelligence testing, society tends to say they are not "smart." That definition of smart is limited, and it leads to the additional challenge of low expectations.

I have rejoiced in the fact that I am smart in ways that people can really relate to. These are some of the ways people have described me: *articulate, emotionally savvy, magnetic, curious, competitive, funny, creative, persistent,* and *big thinker.* When I asked for input into my book, my friend and mentor, David Thomason, said, "David is an influencer, and a pioneer."

> ### Ability and Disability
>
> We all have our own unique disabilities and abilities. Some are more visible than others. Some come out in what we look like. Others come out in how we talk. Others come out in how we act. So I guess we are all different, in the sense that no two people are the same, but maybe we all share in the same needs and aspirations as human beings. We are alike while not the same. We have equal rights but different aspirations.

I am proud that those who know me can see beyond my condition. At the same time, I am humbled and appreciative that those people also see me as a friend, as a one-of-a-kind individual. They know that a label doesn't say who I am. They don't say, "He's a Down syndrome man." They say, "He has Down syndrome." They see me as a person first. That is what I hope this book will help other people do as well.

But here's a point that sometimes gets overlooked: You have to see yourself as an individual, too. Throughout the years, I have learned that my disability does not control my life. Down syndrome is part of me, and it has a place in my life, but I am the sum of many parts. I am comfortable with who I am. I talk about Down syndrome—a lot—because that's a great way to start the conversation about the myths of limits. I am in charge of my attitude and my life.

BOXES HAVE THEIR USES—AND THEIR LIMITS

One of the ways children learn about the world is by learning the names for things. As they learn more and more about the world, they discover that every separate thing is part of a group of things. Those furry things that move around on legs are called cats or dogs. Those things that have wings and fly are called birds. Those pretty things are called flowers, and those big things with leaves are called trees. Those groups fall into larger groups. Cats, dogs, and birds are animals. Flowers and trees are plants. This stacking of boxes within boxes is orderly and helpful.

We all pretty much agree that the names for things and these groupings are important. But labels, categories, and groups tend to show how things are alike. It's more work—and more rewarding—to seek out ways that things are unique. People who have an extra twenty-first chromosome have a condition with a name, and its name is *Down syndrome*. It affects those of us who have it in similar ways and makes a handy, tidy box of characteristics.

But those special characteristics are influenced by other things, too. Sons and daughters with Down syndrome look like their parents because there are many chromosomes, not just the twenty-first. Each chromosome does its part to make every person the sum of his or her parents' genes. And it gets more complicated from there. People are shaped by where they grow up, how many enriching resources are in their community, the commitment of their parents to nurturing their minds and bodies, where they went to school, and all kinds of random things. We are all alike in that way. In fact, in almost every way that matters, people with Down syndrome are just like people who don't have Down syndrome. We are much more alike than different.

We Are Alike as We Are Different

Here are some things that make me, me: I love science and space. I am a *Star Trek* fan. My confirmation godmother, Joan Nickless, gave me a star in the Milky Way galaxy for my birthday. My cousin Issa Nesnas is a robotics and autonomous systems guru at NASA, and he invited me to visit his lab at the Jet Propulsion Lab in Pasadena, California, where he had robots running around the Mars yard. I enjoy science fiction TV shows and movies. One of my favorite shows on TV is *The Big Bang Theory*. I identify with those guys. I also love watching sports and playing games with my family, especially my brother and brothers-in-law and sister-in-law. I am a typical guy, right? But I am still unique.

And that still leaves room for differences that make us individuals. We humans are much more complex than any category system scientists have created to describe our world. When people see my face, they immediately know I have Down syndrome. But that's all they know for sure. Anything else is a guess or an assumption. That's the limit of that very helpful box labeled *Down syndrome*. As a group, my friends with Down syndrome and I are motivated, creative, optimistic, and positive. So why is it that people feel sorry for us, talk down to us, and behave differently when they meet us? They assume things about us before they know us. Instead of assuming we can do many things, they focus on our disability and assume we can't do many things. That bothers me, and it motivates me to speak up.

OWNING WHO YOU ARE

Now back to the NDSS adult conference in Washington, DC.

"My success and ability to make my dreams come true and have a life like yours was possible thanks to the support of family and the people who believed in me," I told the audience. "Early in my life, my parents discovered my talents and always had expectations of me."

Expectations are important. It has been said that the biggest challenge to people with Down syndrome are the low expectations that others have. I have been lucky to have been raised in a family that set a high standard for learning, manners, behavior, and self-reliance. But at the same time, they knew I sometimes needed different types of support and more patient guidance. Individual learning styles are not unique to people with Down syndrome. Every school has kids who are good at many things and not so good at other things. That's true of people with Down syndrome, too.

I have met people throughout the world. I have gotten to know many of them, and we have talked a lot about abilities and disabilities. That made me realize that no matter who they are or where they come from, every person needs to accept who they are. They need to face challenges but also discover and rejoice in their special abilities.

I believe that the world should do the same for each person. With this book, I want to show how embracing abilities makes everyone's life richer. Embracing abilities makes it possible for everyone to surprise themselves and their communities.

People tell kids they can be anything they want to be. When I was growing up, I wanted to be a person who didn't have Down syndrome. It took me a while to accept that I would always have it. Part of learning to accept it was realizing how many great parts of me have nothing to do with Down syndrome. And then it gets really interesting. I have combined all of the things that I love and do well with my interest in speaking up for myself and others with Down syndrome.

So, I am not a university professor and researcher like my mom. I'm not a physicist and rocket scientist like my dad. I am an inspirational public speaker who happens to have Down syndrome.

INCLUSION IS MY GOAL

In my speech at the NDSS adult summit, I talked about a topic that is important to me and a theme throughout this book—inclusion. Just in my lifetime, the idea of inclusion has grown from an uncommon practice to something that is protected by federal law.

"Remember that many of us young and older adults with Down syndrome have experienced inclusive education, are employed, participate in sports, have social lives, live independently, and are self-sufficient," I told the audience. "We are included in all aspects of our society."

Someone who helped make inclusion possible is Eunice Kennedy Shriver, founder of Special Olympics. She is a role model to me because she always spoke up for others. She asked heads of states, legislators, influential people, athletes, and fans to promote inclusion and dignity in our world. Her words and call for justice resonate in my heart: "The right to play on any playing field? You have earned it. The right to study in any school? You have earned it. The right to have a job? You have earned it. The right to be anyone's neighbor? You have earned it."

For the first time in history, we have a group of young and older adults with Down syndrome whose lives have been shaped more by inclusion than exclusion. We are included in every aspect of our society. We are citizens, and we vote.

Inclusion also means taking part in decisions about our lives and well-being. There's a saying that captures this idea: "Nothing about us without us." We want to be involved. We may not always understand everything right away. We may need help to get a feel for complex topics. But we have goals and dreams. And we have a unique point of view. We are the *only* ones who know what it's like to live with Down syndrome.

I think that as a group, people who live with Down syndrome measure success by how well our human and civil rights are respected. We also measure our success by how we are included in our community and the workplace. Today, in my 40s, I dare to dream about changing the way people think of us—changing perceptions and opening doors for people with disabilities to shine in not only sports, but also the workplace and our communities, as well as at every level of society. I see that it has already started.

A NEW GENERATION OF ACHIEVERS

"This is a good time and an opportunity for all of us to celebrate the many accomplishments of adults with Down syndrome. We have made good progress. Many of the adults among us are living their dreams," I told the audience at the adult summit.

Many in the audience had features similar to mine. Many were friends. Those adults with Down syndrome had enjoyed the opportunity, like me, to grow up among friends and family, to learn, to work, to aspire. It was thrilling to me.

People with Down syndrome attend school, university, or vocational internships. Some of us are employed or self-employed in jobs that we chose. Many are artists, models, and actors. We serve in civic positions with legislators and nonprofit leadership roles.

I have friends with Down syndrome who can play multiple musical instruments and speak more than one language, like Sujeet DeSai and Emmanuel Bishop. My friend Karen Gaffney is well-known as a long-distance swimmer who was able to swim across the English Channel and the width of Lake Tahoe. She is an advocate and president of a foundation, received an honorary doctorate, and gave a TED Talk. Ashley DeRamus, an entrepreneur, fashion designer, singer, and advocate, reached her goal of being the first person with special needs to sing the national anthem in all fifty states. Chris Burke is an actor with Down syndrome who played a leading role in the ABC TV show *Life Goes On* for four seasons. My friend Frank Stephens is an inspirational speaker, actor, and activist who challenges those who believe people with Down syndrome should not be born.

We can be amazing in spite of the challenges we face—and maybe because of the challenges, too. Learning from working hard is a skill that can be used in every part of life.

My friends have done things I haven't. I am not the president of a foundation. I don't own a business. I don't speak any languages other than English. I do not play a musical instrument. And I do not act. But I have broken many barriers for people with Down syndrome in the competitive employment arena. I have worked for the international consulting firm

Booz Allen Hamilton, and I now have my dream job as a community relations specialist in the Government Affairs Department of SourceAmerica, a large national nonprofit based in Vienna, Virginia. You'll hear a lot more about SourceAmerica in later chapters.

I have advocated at the local, state, national, and international levels. I have traveled to fourteen countries, and I am always ready to take my message to any corner of the world. I am a curious man, and I like to learn new things. I follow the news, and I have my own views. In fact, the authors of a book called *Firestarters: How Innovators, Instigators, and Initiators Can Inspire You to Ignite Your Own Life* saw me as an "instigator," someone who forges new paths, transforms perspectives, and breaks barriers. I was featured in that book along with forty other innovators, entrepreneurs, and CEOs.

We have exceeded expectations, opened new doors, and taken surprising paths in life. We have taken the boxes that describe us and stacked them up to reach higher. Our stories are still being told, however, and we still carry the weight of stereotypes. But we didn't invent stereotypes, prejudice, or myths. Humans have always struggled to overcome prejudices about culture, ethnic background, race, religion, and many other things.

The difference is that now we can do something about it.

LIVING LONGER RAISES NEW QUESTIONS

"Right here in this room, we have the knowledge and the brain power to make a difference in the lives of people with Down syndrome," I told the audience. "We all care about the quality of our lives, and I am hoping that now, with more funding for research with a focus on Down syndrome, we may discover new ways to slow down the aging process and at a minimum be able to manage our lives in a way that does not take away our self-respect."

Now forty-two, I am one of the older generation of adults with Down syndrome. Our numbers are growing as we live longer, and science is finding there is a lot to learn about how we age. The summit sought to shed light on issues that we worry about as we enter new phases in our lives.

Our parents are older, too. As I face the future, I know there will be things that I am not prepared to embrace. I am thinking of such events as retiring from work, outliving my parents, losing friends, and having to rely more and more on others in my family and the community. And there's more.

I have learned that having an extra twenty-first chromosome can cause problems later in life. Studies show that one of the main genes responsible for Alzheimer's disease is on the twenty-first chromosome. About half of us with Down syndrome will start to show memory loss by age fifty.[2] That really worries me. I have learned that our physical fitness is at risk without regular exercise. I also have heard about sleep problems that impact overall well-being.

But I also know that scientists believe studying people with Down syndrome can help reveal ways to help solve those problems. I have spoken to researchers who believe my extra chromosome may unlock discoveries that benefit not only those with Down syndrome, but also millions of people throughout the world. Wouldn't that be quite an accomplishment for a group of people who have been included in and protected by law only in the last forty years? I can't wait to tell you more in later chapters.

WE HAVE COME FAR BUT STILL HAVE FAR TO GO

When I was born in 1977, my parents were told that I might not live past twenty-five. It's hard for me to imagine what a parent must feel like when they get news like that. When a baby is born, the focus is on the future. Who will she be? What will he achieve? What will make her happy? What will bring joy to his life? I know my parents had those thoughts.

I don't have kids, but I am an uncle. I know how I feel about my niece and nephew. I have to believe that the dreams for your own children are much more intense, so hearing that your baby may not have a long life must have been horribly painful.

I know my parents must be a little shocked by where my life has taken me. Opportunities that didn't exist when I was born allowed me to surprise them in many ways. And because of who I am, and because of what they taught me, I latched on to those opportunities and made the most of them. My family has supported me in every way, and I will tell you all about it.

But there is no way they could have expected their jaundiced little baby to grow up to be an advocate for people with intellectual disabilities. Or to speak at the National Institutes of Health about the importance of Down syndrome research, testify about competitive employment at the U.S. Senate, and share my story during World Down Syndrome Day at the United Nations.

Maybe at some point they thought I might be part of Special Olympics, which was less than ten years old when I was born. But they could never have dreamed I'd be one of twelve Special Olympics athletes chosen to represent the global organization from 2014 to 2018. As a Sargent

Shriver International Global Messenger, I traveled the world, met celebrities, and gave speeches on behalf of Special Olympics.

I can't imagine that they saw me at the center of a truly historic milestone when I was selected as the first-ever Joseph P. Kennedy Jr. Public Policy Fellow with an intellectual disability. When I was a baby, I flailed on the floor just learning to crawl. And I ended up walking the halls of Capitol Hill as part of the Ways and Means Social Security Subcommittee of the House of Representatives.

I will tell you more about that in a later chapter, but for someone like me who enjoyed watching C-SPAN as a boy, being on Capitol Hill was an amazing opportunity. I learned to be an advocate for people with intellectual disabilities long before the fellowship. Thus, I took every opportunity to tell people my thoughts about human and civil rights for all people. I was a reminder to those around me that people with intellectual disabilities do not have to hide.

WISE WORDS FROM SCIENCE OFFICER SPOCK

As I mentioned, I am a huge *Star Trek* fan. My favorite character is Science Officer Spock. As a Vulcan, he was different from most of the human crew. He acted in ways they didn't always understand. I wonder if I was drawn to him because I was different in the eyes of so many people around me. But I also think I was drawn to Spock because he was strong and knew what he had to do to get things done. He was very clear about his mission. He used his ability—logic—to protect his crewmates. They may have seen his lack of emotion as a disability, but it helped him get everyone out of tight spots.

Another thing Spock said was, "Live long and prosper." That's an important idea that I will be talking about in this book. Living long is not enough. We need to prosper, too.

You can't prosper when you are hemmed in by other people's expectations. Remember all of the limits for people with Down syndrome that turned out to be myths. You can replace myths with the truths that you find for yourself, about yourself.

The one thing I would like you to walk away with after reading this book is also inspired by *Star Trek*. I want you to believe that no matter who you are, you can "boldly go where no one has gone before."

1

A FAMILY'S DETERMINATION

> I met David shortly after my first child Arlo was born. Arlo's
> Down syndrome diagnosis had floored me, mostly because I
> had never met anyone with the condition. David was like a
> ray of sunshine. Not only did he offer a glimpse of how spec-
> tacular my son's future could be, he became my first friend
> with Down syndrome. We advocate together, celebrate to-
> gether. He has become part of my life as a peer, an equal. He
> is paving the way so my son's generation can be truly included
> without having to fight so hard for it.
>
> —Erin Croyle, writer and journalist[1]

Things were not easy for my parents when I was born in 1977. They were graduate students in Madison, Wisconsin. They were pursuing PhDs at Wisconsin University, where they first met. Dad was studying nuclear engineering, and Mom was studying educational psychology. I am pretty sure they had not planned on having a baby in the midst of their studies.

I was a surprise first child. That's a challenge to start with. I was born with Down syndrome, and that was also an unexpected surprise. Neither of my parents had ever met anyone with Down syndrome or even with an intellectual disability. Almost everything about me was new to them. They were not prepared.

Society was not prepared, either. Their baby was born into a world where people with intellectual disabilities were rarely seen in public and seldom regarded as worthwhile. The phrase used to describe our condition—*mentally retarded*—was ugly and demeaning. Even the clinical word used to describe people with Down syndrome—*mongoloid*—was offensive and racist.

1

New civil rights laws had already lifted up and empowered many parts of U.S. society, but those laws did not address society's attitudes toward me and others with intellectual disabilities. The idea of having someone like me learning in a regular classroom in a public school wasn't even on the table then. *Mainstreaming* and *inclusion* were uncommon terms, even in the disability community. Mom and Dad were highly educated people who wanted to work in complicated and challenging fields. Whatever dreams they had for their first child changed suddenly on September 17, 1977.

"MY BABY IS BEAUTIFUL"

My mom has often told me the story of the day of my birth. It was early fall in Madison. The leaves were turning warm colors and falling to the ground. It was breezy and sunny, a beautiful day. She was thirty-three years old and ready to be done with an eighteen-hour delivery. My dad was a "super coach" who had attended Lamaze classes with my mother so they would be well-trained and ready for the delivery. The night before my birth, St. Mary's Hospital had been busy with ten other deliveries. There were lots of happy couples and crying babies, and nuns and nurses tending to both with contented professionalism.

I made my entrance into the world crying, like every other baby. I was a solid six pounds, eleven ounces. Happy couple, crying baby. Just like everyone else. But the nurses showed signs that something was different. Something was wrong.

Moments after I was born, my mom could see concern in the faces of the nurses and doctor. That planted an uncertain fear in my new mom. As she remembers it, their gowns were growing whiter, more antiseptic, and their faces were turning pale. The joy my mom felt began to be tinged with confusion and worry. The nurses gathered around me, fussing with me, retreating little by little from my mom's bed, fading away, talking in quiet, urgent terms, and escaping eye contact.

Finally, they took me away. The room was silent.

My parents were alone, uncertain, and unprepared. After what felt like an eternity, the doctor came back and told my parents, "Your son has Down syndrome. I am so sorry."

After a moment of silence, my mom replied, "My baby is beautiful."

The next words they heard were, "We will have someone from social services come talk to you."

My mom then asked to see pictures of children and adults with Down syndrome. She felt a need to meet people with Down syndrome to see what they were like. There were no photos of any babies who looked like me. I am told that a first child is a mother's dream, so why were there no pictures of happy mothers with their babies with Down syndrome? While I was away being examined, my mom was hearing nothing but kind words that weren't at all helpful in understanding what she and Dad would be facing.

The news of my condition was hard on both of my parents. My mom did not believe the nurses or doctors and was in denial. My dad was in tears. He left the hospital that afternoon and returned to our apartment.

Down Syndrome 101

Down syndrome, or trisomy 21, is a genetic condition in which a person is born with three copies of chromosome 21 instead of two. That extra chromosome affects every cell in my body. It's not hereditary; it's a problem that occurs in the womb. People with Down syndrome have many physical features in common, but the most distinctive may be our eyes, which are a bit almond-shaped. Down syndrome causes intellectual disability. There's a wide range of ability in people with Down syndrome, just as there is a wide range of ability in everyone. Oh, and Down syndrome is named for a British man named John Langdon Down, who named the condition that bears his name in 1862. The name has nothing to do with up or down, but it definitely has its ups and downs.

He started calling family, relatives, and friends to share the news. He heard many people say, "I'm sorry," but no one said, "Congratulations." He remembers that to this day.

Everyone my dad talked to on the day I was born genuinely had good intentions. They wanted to help and be supportive but felt awkward about congratulating him. To show support, that afternoon my paternal grandmother drove from Illinois to Wisconsin to help.

My dad couldn't sleep when he went home that day. He returned to the hospital to spend the night in the empty bed next to my mom. The nun in charge said it was fine, as the extra bed was not being used by another mother. She understood that my parents needed some privacy and needed to hug and talk. The unknown is always scary, and maybe they did not know what to think or say. They were at a loss for words. My mom said she felt guilty and asked my dad if he wanted to leave her. He was astonished she would even think about it.

Remember, this was the 1970s. People like me were sent to institutions in those days. We were supposed to be *hidden*, put away, and forgotten. And that is what the folks from social services recommended. My parents turned them down flat. I was their baby, their first child, and they would love and care for me.

That decision has made all the difference in my life. I will always love them for that.

Their decision made a difference in their relationship, too. They bonded that evening after deciding to take their little bundle home, love him, and give him the best care they could. They became stronger together. They were given a mission and were determined to make it work.

ONE BIG CHALLENGE AND MANY LITTLE ONES

The shock of my Down syndrome diagnosis was still fresh and present in the minds of my stunned parents, but they knew now that I was theirs to take care of forever. And there were concerns to deal with right away. Down syndrome or not, I was their baby, and they were focused on what I needed.

I arrived two weeks early, and I was yellow from jaundice because my liver was still a bit underdeveloped. I had to spend quite a bit of time at the hospital out of my mother's arms under special lights in an incubator. The doctors determined that I also had a congenital heart defect typical of babies with Down syndrome. Mine is called a ventricular septal defect (VSD). It's a hole in the wall between the heart's lower chambers. The doctors used a catheter to check the size of the hole and did not think surgery was needed. They monitored me closely to see if the hole would close by itself or stay the same small size. By the time I was ready to leave the hospital, the doctors were confident the heart defect was small enough that I would be okay. Although I received jaundice treatment at the hospital, I was still yellowish when my parents took me home.

At our house in Wisconsin, my mom would put me naked on

> **My Heart**
>
> That little hole in my heart has stayed with me, but it didn't keep me from a very active childhood and a life of sport and exercise. I remember many visits to the cardiologist throughout my life—every month in the first year, then every three months, then once a year, and now once every three years. My hole never got bigger, and my heart grew stronger, so no surgery was ever needed. I still get it checked every three years.

a blanket next to the window where there was good sunlight to help me regain strength. She would also nurse me, and that was hard, as I would constantly fall asleep. I lost quite a bit of weight and was down to five pounds. It took a while to regain weight and begin to grow steadily. My parents worked hard figuring out a way to give me a boost. During the next few months, I improved, but I kept having a sharp cough from the croup. I had to be taken to the hospital a few times to sleep in an oxygen tent while the infection played out. Despite everything, I started to thrive, and slowly but surely I grew stronger.

A COMMUNITY OF SUPPORT

Many of my parents' friends came to visit and meet me. My mom and dad's family traveled many miles to spend time with me. They all saw me as a beautiful, happy baby. In Wisconsin, we lived in a friendly neighborhood near campus where people checked on one another and were willing to help. We also had friends from the university who were part of our community of support. People gave me lots of gifts, especially stuffed animals. I got all kinds of bears and puppies, but my favorite was Bucky the Badger, the official mascot of the University of Wisconsin–Madison. I still have him after all these years, and my four-year-old nephew Mason and my niece Mira play with him.

My parents were graduate students with demanding requirements for becoming doctoral candidates. Having a child with Down syndrome was stressful and time-consuming. My mom took a break from her studies and dedicated herself to taking care of me. My dad slowed down his research as well to provide support.

Being born on a university campus had lots of advantages. We were surrounded by brilliant and caring minds, curious folks who enjoyed pursuing solutions to problems. Access to the best doctors was easy. For example, a few months after my birth, my parents and I met with Dr. John M. Opitz, a famous, tall, and slender geneticist at the University of Wisconsin. He was the first celebrity I met in my life.

During our visit, Dr. Opitz held me so that my entire body fit perfectly in his big hand. He had the largest and longest hands, and he used them to slowly and meticulously identify the forty-four physical traits of a person with Down syndrome.

I showed all of the traits of a typical baby with Down syndrome, so there was no question about my diagnosis, even before the blood test that confirmed it. My dad was interested in learning all of the details. I think it was too much for my mom, however. She did not want me to be an object of diagnosis.

Although Dr. Opitz is widely known for identifying and discovering genetic disorders, he said identifying genetic syndromes was never his main goal. Rather, he said, "My goal simply was to care for the patients and their families."[3]

When my mom asked if she would be likely to have more babies with Down syndrome or other conditions, he responded that at her age, the chances were very high. But he gave her a grin and said, "It would be selfish not to have more kids. David needs siblings." (I am glad my parents followed that good advice. I have three younger siblings now.)

A Star in Medical Genetics

Dr. Opitz was a pioneer in the study of how genetics affect the human body. He began his residency and then completed his fellowship in pediatrics at the University of Wisconsin soon after graduating from the University of Iowa in 1959. He studied under Klaus Patau, PhD, a plant cytogeneticist, and David W. Smith, MD, a pediatric endocrinologist who is considered the father of dysmorphology—the study of structural defects, particularly congenital malformations in people. Dr. Smith introduced Dr. Opitz to a facility in Wisconsin where children and adults with severe mental disabilities lived. Soon thereafter, he began his life's work of learning to recognize physical and biological signs and symptoms of disorders. Dr. Opitz founded the *American Journal of Medical Genetics* in 1976, becoming its first editor in chief and remaining in that position until 2001. The first volume appeared in 1977, the year I was born.[2]

My mom was new to motherhood and knew nothing about it. She was scared of the unknown and worried about what people thought. I was tiny, and she did not want strangers to ask her too many questions—How old is he? Is he nursing? Is he your first baby?—when she took me to the store or park. I looked three months old when I was five months old. Her initial fear and sense of isolation were quickly transformed into determination. She believed in her child's ability to be happy and have a life worth living, a life that matters, a life like anyone else, a life of his own, and a life that would leave a mark wherever he goes.

MY LIFE IN PICTURES

My parents have told me many stories about the early days of my childhood. They have six albums of me from the first two years of my life. (My brother, Marc, who is twelve years younger than me, doesn't have any!) Mom had a playgroup that met once or twice a week at our apartment. One of the children there was born on the same day as I was and in the same hospital, and his dad was a colleague of my mom's. The others were children of graduate students who lived close by. Based on these photos, which I've seen countless times, I was happy to be surrounded by my peers even though they were bigger and stronger than I was. They would crawl all over the place, and I would try hard to mimic their actions, even if I could not keep up with them. I enjoyed the playgroup and must have learned a lot. I had fun.

In that first year of my life, my parents were consumed by paying attention to every detail to ensure my well-being. I was baptized at home by the same two Catholic priests who married my parents at St. Paul's University Catholic Church at the University of Wisconsin. Believers and nonbelievers attended the ceremony, which was followed by great food and camaraderie. My mom's PhD advisor, Professor M. Vere DeVault, was named my godfather. My mother's best friend and first roommate at the university, Alice Woll Erickson, was named my godmother. Alice is still a good friend of the family and stays in touch. Professor DeVault has passed away. The group of friends who came to the baptism are still friends today and come from several different countries. I am glad that I was exposed to an international community early on in my life.

My pediatrician, Dr. Ordean Torstenson, was also a wonderful person. He helped me by teaching my parents ways to get my strength back after losing so much weight. It was good for them to get his advice about things they could do right away to help me. Dr. Torstenson showed them that in most ways, I was like other babies. I could get stronger, and they could help.

EXPERTS IN OUR OWN BACKYARD

It helped to have world-class experts in child development nearby. Those experts were at the Waisman Research Center, part of the University of Wisconsin. Early in my childhood, I was a subject of research by physical therapists, occupational therapists, and speech and language specialists. The researchers wanted to watch me as I developed because they could look at the way I grew and learn something about the way other people developed. (I happily went along with this as a baby and toddler, but I have chosen to be involved in research in my adult years, as you will see in a later chapter.)

There were hidden benefits to my parents having these experts close by and involved. For the first time, they found out they could improve many of the things that made me different from kids my age who didn't have Down syndrome. Those other kids progressed through stages of development quicker than I did and with less focused help.

But I did make progress. I went from swimming in place on the floor to crawling (to walking, to running, to swimming, to playing baseball, to playing basketball—stories for later). Two researchers, Dr. Ana Doodlah and her student Rita Holstein, were also experts in muscle movement and physiology. They taught my parents exercises to help but also why those exercises were helpful. For two parents who yearned to know the reasons why things happen in the world (especially my dad), that knowledge was a gift. When you understand something better, you fear it less. When you can look at something big and seemingly impossible as a bunch of smaller, doable things, you start to feel a sense of control and accomplishment. That's what happened. Down syndrome started to feel like something they could handle. Every new thing they learned to manage was one less thing to worry about.

I was just a baby, untroubled by any of those grown-up concerns. But I learned, too. My dad put my favorite toys just out of reach, and I struggled to move to get to them. Every time I was able to get my muscles to move together and lurch forward, I was learning about doing things for myself. That's something my parents did on purpose, right from the start. They wanted me to learn to help myself and not feel helpless. They had taken on big challenges in their lives, and they wanted me to feel comfortable with taking on challenges, too. Learning to crawl was lesson one of many.

> **The Bean Connoisseur**
>
> Rita Holstein, from the Waisman Research Center, started working with me when I was twelve months old. She focused on my fine motor skills, which involve the little muscles in my hands and fingers. Grasping and picking up things was one of those skills. As an exercise, she laid out raisins and beans for me to pick up. It was difficult for me to pick up those pesky raisins. I was nicknamed the "Bean Connoisseur," as I could only grab the green beans. Rita would also ask me to build towers out of blocks. In some research note somewhere, it shows I very much preferred throwing blocks to stacking them. It was a hard task but worth the effort, as I "picked it up" as time passed.

JUST ONE OF THE KIDS

My mom was off from work during these crucial first months of my life. She read to me every day. *Winnie the Pooh* and *Goodnight Moon* were our favorite books to read together. She spent lots of time with me and was always searching for opportunities that would benefit me. The playgroup was fun, but it was getting to be time for my mom to get back to work on her PhD.

She asked around for recommendations for a nursery school near us. That's how she heard about Kiddie Camp, a place for kids with intellectual disabilities. Mom and Dad decided to try it out. It was a half-day program, and Mom would drive me to the camp. She says dropping me off was hard on her. She would peek through the windows to watch what I was doing inside. I was a happy kid, and the teachers were kind. There are photos of me reaching out when Mrs. Goussman would blow bubbles for me to catch.

I look happy in the photos, but Mom was not satisfied and felt that it wasn't the right environment for me. In my playgroup at home, I had

> **A Good Idea, Then and Now**
>
> The Waisman Early Childhood Program has grown from having twelve kids in one classroom to being an accredited preschool. It serves one hundred fifty kids in six classrooms. The school has a variety of staff and professionals dedicated to full inclusion, and they give children a great start in life no matter their diagnosis and condition. Every child is gifted in some way or another. The earlier you explore their talents, the sooner their abilities surge and blossom. I believe I am good proof that it works.

been with kids my same age. None of them had any kind of disability, and we played together just fine. That had been really good for me. Having only kids with intellectual disabilities at Kiddie Camp bothered my parents. The teachers there were great, but I wasn't learning as much from my peers. My mom and dad wanted me to learn as much as I could and be in an environment that challenged me. They decided to keep searching.

In the fall of 1979, when I was two years old, the Waisman Early Childhood Program opened.[4] It came together based on interest from parents and children in the community, educational institutions, and professionals in education. The goal was to have a high-quality childcare and early education program that served children with special needs without isolating them. This was a new idea in the 1970s, and it was called *mainstreaming*. The program benefitted families who wanted a rich education for their little ones. It was also a place for professionals to learn and shape the practice of mainstreaming.

My parents agreed that this was bound to be a better approach, and they were happy to work with the center to make me part of that new program.

The first class was made up of twelve kids. There were ten more or less typically developing kids plus me, with Down syndrome, and another kid with autism. We had two teachers. One had a background in early childhood education, and the other had a special education background. Both of them worked with all of us. I loved the program, and it was good for me. We had drama, free play, blocks and trucks, music, field trips, and many other activities with our great teachers. They cared for each one of us. They even remembered me years later when I came back to visit.

MY SISTER, MY ROLE MODEL

Three years after I was born, my sister Teresa was born. She weighed nine pounds, ten ounces at birth and looked three months old when Mom brought her home from the hospital. My parents say that everything came easy for her. She was talking at fifteen months, and at eighteen months she wanted to join me in the Waisman Early Childhood Program. The minimum age was two, but they made an exception for her. She flourished there, just as I did.

I would give her big hugs and squeeze her hard to let her know how much I loved her. I learned so much from Teresa as we grew up together. She developed skills quickly. It wasn't long before she was able to do things I couldn't yet do. She became my role model, and I imitated her as much as I could. I wanted to do everything she did. And she did a lot. We would go together to the park across from where we lived on Mendota Lake. It was great living close to the lake. Teresa loved the water and had no fear of walking into the lake. Mom sometimes had to run in after her to make sure she did not go in too deep. Our neighbor, a professor at the university, had a sailboat, and he would take us sailing on weekends.

Life was good in Madison. We had lots of friends and supporters. My family was determined to have me succeed. The integration and acceptance they found for me in that community helped a lot. My parents had been unprepared for the unexpected. They were speechless at first and at a loss. Having a child with Down syndrome had felt like a bombshell, a crash into the unknown. But as soon as they established a routine and found methods that proved to be effective, we all thrived together. They set a goal of providing me with a life full of love. In fact, I would say that they gave me an *extraordinary* life full of love and opportunities. Our great start in Madison was a big part of that.

When my dad got a job in Washington, DC, we had to leave Madison. That marked a turning point for all of us—in many ways.

CHALLENGES

The move to the DC area and later to the little town of Vienna brought good opportunities in the long run, but there were a few challenges. I had some good and some not-so-good teachers. The transition to Vienna started out wobbly and ended well. I have great memories of a wonderful teacher there who understood inclusion and was willing to take a few risks to make sure that I and others in my class had a chance to be integrated with our peers. (I tell that story later.)

Transitions are the milestones and turning points that involve new people, places, and situations. I've had a few of those crucial and interesting experiences throughout my life's journey. These transitions were growth experiences for me and our entire family.

I give my parents and everyone who has accompanied me on my journey a high five and an A+ for effort. Everyone was determined to see me succeed. They helped me beat the odds. We proved so many people wrong about the capabilities of people with Down syndrome.

There's a lesson I've learned in my life that is worth sharing: I want every parent of a child with disabilities to know that if they believe in themselves and their child, they will find ways to do things as a team that might surprise the world—and themselves. Challenges are opportunities in disguise, but you have to meet those challenges and try—and maybe fail—before you can really see the challenges in context.

What seems like an obstacle or hurdle may become a chance to take a new path that didn't reveal itself at first. You can beat the odds by recognizing that the "odds" are based on what others have done before. An unlikely outcome can be made more likely through persistence and determination. And remember that some barriers are based on assumptions. When you test an assumption—when you give it a good poke or a rattling shake—sometimes the assumption falls apart and you find it's not a barrier at all.

My parents were told about all kinds of barriers I could face in my life. So were many other parents whose children with Down syndrome ended up in institutions. They were kept in place by sterile concrete walls and the low expectations of society. Only one of those barriers was real.

2

IMAGINING THE POSSIBILITIES

David implored my colleagues to include people with disabilities in our work, speaking movingly about the importance of working with—not about—people with disabilities to tell a different story, a story about what is possible.

—Nicki Pombier Berger, oral historian[1]

My family has always imagined the possibilities for me throughout my life. I was born in the 1970s. Society at that time did not offer people with intellectual disabilities many options. That didn't stop my parents from looking for opportunities for me. And when an opportunity didn't exist, they tried to create it, one way or another.

Early on, they thought about where I should go to school. The options varied a little but not much. Education laws were different from state to state. School systems were different from county to county. And how laws and policies were used could be different even from school to school.

Everywhere my mom and dad looked, choices for me were limited. But their hopes for me never were. We've come a long way since then. Thanks to the work of many, we are more accepting of differences. When Congress reauthorized the Individuals with Disabilities Education Act (IDEA) in 2004, and

Inclusion Is More Common Today

Today, many educators believe that inclusion in the classroom is important. They understand that students both with and without disabilities benefit in meaningful ways. Families nowadays still have to work hard to make sure their children with disabilities are included in regular classrooms. We're getting there. But we still could do better.

amended it in 2015, through public law 114-95, the Every Student Succeeds Act, Congress stated,

> Disability is a natural part of the human experience and in no way diminishes the rights of individuals to participate in or contribute to society. Improving educational results for children with disabilities is an essential element of our national policy of ensuring equality of opportunity, full participation, independent living, and economic self-sufficiency for individuals with disabilities.[2]

This welcoming point of view was not widely held as I was growing up. Most people with disabilities were taught in schools or classrooms that were separate from other students. The practice of inclusion, which is meaningful integration of people with and without disabilities in a classroom, was rare. That meant that other students, teachers, and administrators didn't see what people with intellectual disabilities could do in school. It did nothing to make people aware of our abilities. We were seen as a problem to be fixed outside of the mainstream.

Nowadays, inclusion is encouraged by law, and many people see its advantages. As part of the inclusion process, each student with a disability has an individualized education plan (or IEP). The IEP lays out their school goals and lists the supports they need to learn. With good teachers at a school that believes in the power of inclusion, students with IEPs learn in the environment that suits them best. For some, it's a small classroom with few distractions. For others, it's a regular classroom with regular students. That's what the "I" in IEP is all about: individualization.

INCLUSION WAS RARE IN THE 1970S

It's great what's happening now, but in the late 1970s and early 1980s, few schools planned thoughtfully for teaching people with intellectual disabilities. There were laws that students with disabilities should be taught in the "least restrictive environment." Identifying what that is for every student isn't easy, however. Principals and teachers often disagree with parents, and parents, like mine, often feel that school leaders underestimate what their children can do. When educators looked at people like me, they saw the faces of people with Down syndrome. They might have seen children behaving in ways that seemed odd. Few people took the time to look past first appearances. They assumed the worst instead of treating each of us as individuals with strengths and needs.

My parents saw it differently. They believe that each child is unique. Some kids are tall, and some are short. Some are good at math, and others are great at writing. Some love science and history, and some prefer art and writing. It's the same way with people with disabilities. When students with special needs were taught separately, it was easy for educators to think we all had the same needs and abilities. My parents saw me growing up, and they learned that an intellectual disability still leaves lots of room for personality and achievement. My parents believe that every child has untapped potential and a need to be discovered and stimulated in a natural environment.

Every individual has their own preferred learning style. For example, some people learn well just from listening. Other people learn through reading. Others might need to touch and feel things to understand. Kids with special needs also have differing learning styles. If a child has an intellectual disability, they will learn more slowly and usually need more repetition. *Special needs* is just another way to say "different needs." My needs were different, and my mom and dad did what they could to make sure my needs were met.

Changing Laws May Not Change Minds

Because of the Education for All Handicapped Children Act (EHA) in 1975, public schools had to work with and around the needs of every child with a disability. The law required school leaders to work with families to create IEPs for each student. The goal of the law was to teach people with disabilities the same as students without disabilities, or as close as possible. My parents and I discovered that having a law like that helped, but it didn't mean schools always tried hard to make my education equal to my peers without disabilities.

Let's Talk about Placement

Inclusion works differently for different students. Some students learn best in a classroom with a few others who need one-on-one help and a quiet place to learn. But for many students with intellectual disabilities, being in a classroom with mainstream students is where they learn best. As you can imagine, families and educators often disagree about proper placement. It's a conversation that can seem like a battle, with strong opinions on both sides. Maybe it is because we do not have enough data to make the case.

LAWS ABOUT EDUCATION BEGAN TO CHANGE

Most parents of children with disabilities probably learn that lesson. Most probably believe their children should be given a fair chance at a good education. It took a long time for people in power to see things that way. Just getting to the point where schools had to plan education around a student's individual abilities took years of hard work and changes in national laws.

Education was an important aspect of the Civil Rights Movement that led to the formation of the EHA in 1975.[3] Earlier, President John F. Kennedy, thanks to his sister Eunice, "brought intellectual disabilities 'out of the shadows' and into the public light."[4] These years were marked by strife in the United States, from the assassination of President Kennedy in 1963, to the Vietnam War, which lasted until 1975. In addition to those events, the Civil Rights Movement was in full force. Education was soon at the forefront of many political agendas.[5]

Fifteen years later, in 1990, EHA was replaced by IDEA. The point of IDEA was to take a balanced look at the strengths and needs of each student instead of focusing so much on their disabilities. IDEA went much further than the earlier EHA. It promoted research and technology development to help students learn better. It outlined programs to help students with their lives after high school. One of the most important changes in the law required that children be taught in their neighborhood schools instead of sending them to separate schools that were only for students with disabilities.[6]

Having students with all kinds of disabilities in the same school is an essential aspect of inclusion. But inclusion is not just having students with disabilities in the same building with mainstream students or even in the same classroom. It's about finding the place and method that allows each student to learn their best.

As I said earlier, few places were welcoming enough to mix people with disabilities into classrooms in the 1970s. Luckily, my family lived in Madison, Wisconsin. The Madison community was open to inclusion when my parents made inquiries. In 1979, the Waisman Research Center was looking into creating an early childhood program and reached out to my family. I, along with another kid with autism, was the first child to be fully included in the newly created center at the Waisman Center with ten other preschoolers. That experience was a rewarding part of my early education and laid the foundation for my social skills and overall development.

OUR NEW HOME IN VIRGINIA

Moving from Wisconsin to our new home in Virginia was a challenge. We had lived in the welcoming academic university town of Madison and were settling in the busy Washington, DC, area. What an adjustment. We lived just outside the capital in Virginia. The city and its suburbs were bigger in every way. The area was full of people from throughout the United States and the world. Traffic was awful. The Madison summers were milder than the hot, humid Augusts of Washington. At least the DC winters were not so cold.

We also had to adjust to new schools and a new set of people with whom to live, work, and play. My dad moved to the Washington, DC, area before we did. He wanted to get a feel for the area and find schools that welcomed people with intellectual disabilities among their students. My mom and dad rented a place in Falls Church, Virginia, a little city right outside Washington. I went to kindergarten at Mount Daniel Elementary School. Both of my parents insisted that I continue to be fully integrated in the school. The school welcomed me and provided some extra help to accommodate my pace of learning. Other kids needed help, too, so we were alike in that way. I was lucky that teachers and school leaders in Madison and Falls Church treated me as an individual. I had special needs, but that was just part of who I was. I learned and played with my peers. It didn't matter if they had disabilities.

LEARNING HOW TO LEARN WITH OTHERS

One thing that made my kindergarten time at Mount Daniel successful was the way my parents taught me and my siblings about getting along with others. My parents wanted all of their children to learn good social skills while we were little. It's just as important to learn to communicate and be polite and patient as it is to read and add numbers. And children need to learn how to behave and play with others early in childhood. Being a good citizen who belongs and is responsible are crucial skills to learn early in life. My parents are not alone in their beliefs.

Many early childhood educators agree that social and emotional development are just as important for a successful school experience as cognitive development. This development begins before the child ever sets foot in a classroom and continues unabated throughout their entire academic career. Kindergarten is a particularly important period for this area of development; it's where the foundational skills for appropriate social behavior are learned and embedded.

My parents wanted me to learn how to play (and work) with others, but I also learned to care about others. It's easy for anyone to be selfish, but learning that other people have feelings and needs just like mine made me less selfish (usually). It's hard to learn those things when you're not mixing with all kinds of children.

> **Learning Independence**
>
> One of the most important things I learned as a child was to try to solve problems myself. My parents let me try and fail, and that's how I learned to not give up when something got in my way. I learned how to read and follow instructions instead of waiting for other people to help me. People often underestimate me, so figuring out how to do things myself was important.

THE LIFE OF A PRIMARY SCHOOL STUDENT

I was at Mount Daniel for two years of kindergarten and first grade, learning and playing along with the other students. I was the only child with special needs in my class, and I did just fine. I learned how to share and make friends. Just like the other kids, I learned how to do things for myself. I learned what all the other kids learned about being good students and good citizens. I was happy and made friends easily. My best friend was my neighbor, Pedro, whose family was from Chile. We swam together and pestered my sister, Teresa. And I mixed right in there in kindergarten at Mount Daniel. I was the oldest kid, but I was small enough to not stand out as different from the other kids. I got extra help; I would visit with Mrs. Reeves, the special education teacher, for one-on-one academic subjects three times a week. The good thing was that I was not the only one who left the classroom for sessions like that. Other kids did, too.

I am a very social guy. I like meeting people and making friends. Pedro was my neighbor, and Billy was the son of a family friend. They were my best friends. They both would visit my house. We liked to play with my younger sister Teresa, who was their age. Pedro liked to take her stuffed animals from her bedroom and throw them down to the first floor in our townhouse. He then would run down the stairs and hide them in the family room and toy room. It was fun going up and down those stairs.

I learned a lot from being around Teresa and neighborhood friends. Learning was easy for Teresa. I looked up to her. She did things I couldn't do. I learned that by trying and practicing, I could do many of those things, too. Those feelings of being included in everyday school and neighborhood life came to an end when our rental ended unexpectedly. We moved nearby but just outside of the Falls Church city school system. When we left the city of Falls Church, we left behind more than friends. We also left behind the welcoming inclusiveness of my school. It took a long time to find it again.

UNWELCOME IN THE CLASSROOM

Our new neighborhood was called Shrevewood. Teresa and I went to the neighborhood school there. We had a new sister, Miranda, who was born in October 1986, when I was nine. Mom, Dad, Teresa, Miranda, and I lived in a big house on a circle. We loved the neighborhood and easily made friends. Our neighbors, the La Salle family, had three kids. Their oldest daughter was the same age as Teresa. We did a lot together, roller skating around the circle and playing with Miranda. She was like a doll to all of us, although we played with her carefully. My friends Pedro and Billy would visit and join in the fun in our big backyard. Life at home was lots of fun.

It was a different story at school. Shrevewood Elementary School was in Fairfax County, so it was part of that public-school system. It was a much bigger system, and they did things differently from the Falls Church city schools. The result for me was a kind of isolation. For the first time, I didn't feel like I was included with the other kids. I was in second grade, and I had to sit in the back of the classroom. As long as I behaved, the teacher let me sit there, and she ignored me. I was not involved and learning. I was in the classroom but was not included in the class as the other children were. I felt left out. That didn't feel good.

When I returned home each day my first week, Mom would ask, "How was your day, David? What did you do?"

And every day, I replied, "Nothing."

Mom was not pleased. She asked for a meeting with the teacher. To our surprise, the teacher said that I needed an IEP before she would do anything with me. She also added that I did not have the paperwork to qualify for it and would need to go to a special school that had services for people like me. My parents were disappointed with her responses. After several inquiries, we found out that kids with special needs in the Fairfax County school system were bused to centers throughout the county. (This was before IDEA of 1990 required children with disabilities to be taught in their neighborhood schools.) Vienna Elementary School was recommended as one of the best in the county. But Vienna was a long bus ride from Falls Church. I wouldn't be with my neighborhood friends at school. Even so, my family decided to do what was best for me, and we moved again. (We haven't moved since then.)

INCLUSION SNAGS IN ELEMENTARY SCHOOL

The third, fourth, and fifth grades were not as much fun as my earlier schooling. Educators used IEPs to determine if you would be in a "trainable" special education class or a "mildly retarded" special education self-contained classroom. (The terms used then were different and uglier than what we use today.) In both cases, students with intellectual disabilities were kept apart from most other students. In most schools, inclusion was not seen as a workable way to teach. No one was happy about the situation, but there were no other options at the time. My parents looked into private schools, but none would allow me to be in the classroom and give extra help on the side.

I was ten when I went to Vienna Elementary School in 1987. The first year at Vienna Elementary School was not what we had imagined, expected, or hoped for. My teacher did not like my inquisitive, opinionated nature. She got me and my family into trouble. And of all things, the trouble had to do with baseball.

Ever since I began to crawl, I loved all activities and sports involving a ball. Baseball was my dad's favorite childhood sport and pastime, like many of his generation, and he would practice with me. He ran me through all the rules, and we practiced the basics of throwing, catching, and batting. My old man trained me the best he could. We would often watch the games together on TV and practice in the backyard when I got home from school. Funny enough, my dad and I maybe practiced a little too hard.

One time when we were playing catch, I was not paying attention or maybe was using my glove wrong. The ball missed my glove and hit me squarely in the face, giving me a nice black eye. If you can picture it, I wore these large '80s-style prescription glasses that covered the majority of my little face. The whole thing was a mess, but I got cleaned up and kept on trucking.

When I went to school the next day, my teacher asked me what happened. I said, "No worries, my dad hit me with the baseball." I thought that cleared up the situation pretty well, but, in fact, it was the start of a whole new ballgame. My teacher reported my badly bruised eye, and I guess she gave the wrong impression when she called child social services.

They responded to her accusations and knocked at our door. It took a while to discover they were responding to a reported case of child abuse. It took much longer to sort out what had happened and clear my parents of any suspicion of mistreating me.

Things never got better with that fifth grade teacher. I was too mischievous, stubborn, and opinionated. She wanted me to sit quietly, but I asked too many questions for her taste. She had low expectations of my ability to learn. Yet, she didn't like it when I spoke my mind. She didn't care for my dad, either, after he told her he didn't agree with her teaching style.

My teacher and I argued in the classroom, so she sent me to the principal's office almost every day. But Robert Pantall, the principal, was a good guy, and we liked each other. I enjoyed visiting him, and I wanted my teacher to send me to his office. Mr. Pantall understood me because he had been a special education teacher before becoming a principal. He was my pal.

I know people sometimes don't get along. But I wonder if my fifth grade teacher could have approached things in a different way. My attitudes and opinions showed I was thinking, just not the way she wanted me to. My dad probably had really good ideas about ways to teach me. After all, he and my mom had been teaching me for years, and they knew what worked.

Mr. Pantall Saw Who I Was

My principal, Mr. Pantall, knew I liked to have conversations, and he noticed that I spoke quite well for a child with Down syndrome. I shared with him that I liked to recite poems. So he asked me to prepare one and present it at a school assembly. I did it, and I was so proud. Neither of us knew that I would go on to be a public speaker.

MY WONDERFUL SIXTH GRADE OF INCLUSION

Things took a turn for the better in the fall of 1989. That year, I entered sixth grade and met my favorite teacher, Rachelle Zola. She was the *best*. She was different from the other special education teachers I had at Vienna Elementary because she believed in our abilities and wanted us to interact with other students in the school. She thought it was beneficial for the education of every student.

Ms. Zola's special ed class was similar to others. She taught nine students in her class with the help of a teacher's aide. Our special education class had students of all ages and abilities in one room. My friend, Casey Hammeke, and I were the same age and were the oldest students in our class. We both have Down syndrome and loved playing sports in Special Olympics. We were able to stay in touch and remain friends throughout middle school and high school, and even later, until she moved with her family to North Carolina. I was also friends with her brother Brendan, who also had Down syndrome, and the entire Hammeke family was heavily involved in Special Olympics and the Down syndrome community in Northern Virginia.

Ms. Zola was searching for ways to increase our opportunities to learn. She had a great idea, and after she explained it in a thoughtful and persuasive way, the principal and other teachers in the school supported her initiative. Her idea was something she called a "self-contained classroom with a 'twist.'" The twist was this: Students from the mainstream classes visited our classroom and partnered with us. Individually, we would join in the general education classes when Ms. Zola was sure we would do well, and we were specifically matched with another student in the regular classroom. This was an experiment in inclusion, and Ms. Zola made it happen for us.

I was a sixth grader, so Ms. Zola asked another sixth-grade teacher to have me come into her class during language arts when they were writing and sharing stories. That teacher held her students to a high standard and voiced some skepticism at the request. Ms. Zola assured her I would fit in beautifully. And I did.

The teacher thanked Ms. Zola after the first time I visited her for story writing time. She said that having me in the classroom added a lot and that all of the kids interacted with me in a natural way. A lot of times, people fear inclusion until they see it in action. Ms. Zola really had faith in me, and I am glad I made her proud. During the course of the year, I took on a project with a student from this class to conduct interviews in the community and write stories about what we had learned.

As I always say, Ms. Zola was the best and my favorite teacher, but it did not start out so well. She intrigued me because she was

---

Solving Two Problems at Once

I remember clearly that I did not like to write things by hand. My handwriting was bad, and it took away from the time I was spending interviewing people. I had an idea that solved both problems. I recorded the interviews (I still have that recording device) so I could focus on the person I was talking to.

so different from my other teachers. We connected and have been good friends throughout the years, but it was not "friendly at first sight." As I was writing this book, I asked her to share her memories of being my teacher. The following is her favorite story:

> One day early in the school year I did something or said something that upset David. I don't recall what I said or did, and I do recall, with great fondness, his response. He stood up, threw his desk and chair to the floor. He gave me the best menacing look that an adorable eleven-year-old can give and stomped to the doorway. Standing outside of the room with hands gripping the door jamb he poked his head into the room and said in a stern voice, "I'm going to Mr. Pantall and tell him about you!" Mr. Bob Pantall was the school principal.
>
> I looked at David calmly and said, "Okay, I'll be here when you get back." He continued looking at me and this time said something close to this, "I'm going to Mr. Pantall, and you are going to be in big trouble!" Once again, I let him know I'd be in the room when he got back. He released the door jamb, stood straight, and without saying a word, he walked back into the classroom, picked up his chair, sat down, and got back to work.
>
> I could see that David was in total disbelief. He was looking for a fight, and he didn't get one. I found out after the fact, from Kathleen, his mother, that his previous teacher and he would have verbal arguments. Nothing else was said. Nothing else needed to be said. For me, our interaction that day cemented our relationship, our friendship, that has lasted all these many years—a relationship, a friendship, filled with love and respect.

Ms. Zola concluded,

> David, you were your own "man" then, and I continue to marvel at the man you have grown into. Not only are you a gift to me, you are truly a gift to the world with your loving, knowing message that we are all one. David, you have left an indelible mark on my heart and on the hearts of all those you have touched directly and indirectly.[7]

Ms. Zola complimented me often on my verbal ability: "For David, his vocabulary is an exquisite way to express himself that pushes the boundaries of the stereotype of what it means to be a person with Down syndrome," she said. "When he speaks, people listen. From a very young age, before he was aware of the impact he would have on the world, he has been an advocate for others to find their voices. It is a gift to watch him thrive as he shares himself, his heart with others, and how they respond in kind."[8]

At the time, she was volunteering with the director of fundraising for Special Olympics in Northern Virginia. She decided to take me with them on fundraising outings because she believed I would do a good job representing the area athletes with intellectual disabilities. We met with different civic and business community leaders, and I think we were successful.

Added Ms. Zola,

> The first gathering David spoke at was a Chamber of Commerce meeting, and he was a natural. They loved him! He was totally comfortable speaking in front of strangers. He spoke about his many and varied experiences with Special Olympics, the importance of Special Olympics, and he answered all of their questions. He was an inspiration then, and he continues to be an inspiration now.[9]

Ms. Zola was a great teacher, and she knew that words with lots of syllables were my favorites. She found a great way to teach those big words to me. We would sing a word in a loud voice and then in a soft voice. We would sing it slowly, then sing it fast. We would sing it in a funny voice, emphasizing different syllables. She would use a "baton" as if conducting a choir as I followed along.

A HINT OF THE FUTURE ME ON STAGE

I loved it when I got to be the conductor. In fact, while I liked to be on the stage, I was never into acting. I loved being the emcee, the keynote speaker, and the one in charge. I loved standing up in front of the class to recite poems. I would do it again and again, practicing until I felt it was perfect.

Ms. Zola wrote about that time in this way:

> David, I can still see you standing up in front of the class with your props and reciting the poem over and over again until it was exactly as you wanted it to be. You were animated, and your pure delight with yourself shined through with your great smile. There were times when you had this certain smile, it was as though you had a secret joke going on inside of you and it made you smile to think of it. You weren't always patient with yourself, and in this situation, you were patient, having fun, being playful. You still very much wanted to do it well, and there was no stress. Perhaps it was because your classmates were all

practicing in front of each other, and in your own way, you all gave each other permission to be silly, to make mistakes, and to succeed.[10]

Ms. Zola wrote a book called *Simple Successes: From Obstacles to Solutions with Special Needs Children*.[11] She stressed that each child is capable of learning and wants to learn. She wrote in an email that together "we will find a way for the learning to take place. The emphasis is on what he or she can do. It's a way of seeing the world that we share—while others see obstacles and barriers, we seek and find solutions."[12]

Adding My Thoughts

The greatest honor my sixth grade teacher gave me was when she asked me and my mom to write the foreword to her book. Ms. Zola said she asked me to write the introduction to *Simple Successes* because we share an "I *can do* attitude." I often recommend her book when I speak, especially to educators and parents.

SEEING MY OWN POSSIBILITIES
IN AND AFTER HIGH SCHOOL

I had some good teachers in middle and high school, but none of them had a personality like Ms. Zola. Even so, I had good experiences. I entered middle school in the 1990s. At that time, middle and high school students with special needs were taught in self-contained classrooms. But at my school, McLean High School, I was allowed to be fully included in electives. I was there among the mainstream students in home economics, shop, sex education, and driver's education. I also did wrestling. My teachers were kind. They taught me well and wanted me to succeed. I enjoyed the social studies and science projects, as well as our civics classes. On graduation day, I walked across the stage with my classmates but didn't earn a general education diploma.

In high school, I also had the chance to learn about the world of work through programs run by the county public school system for special needs students. We had a business class, and I did an internship with the National Wildlife Federation during the school year for a few hours three days a week. I also went to the Wilson Center in Staunton, Virginia, for two weeks.[13] The program was created to determine what jobs someone might be good for. I was one of few people with intellectual disabilities to go there. The specialists there tested me for two weeks, test after test. It turned out that I have good administrative office skills.

That first summer after high school, I was offered an internship at the consulting firm Booz Allen Hamilton. When I went to the internship, I got a chance to prove the Wilson Center tests right. I continued my internship a half-day while in post-secondary vocational training at the Davis Career Center for two years.

The internship was a great example of what can happen when

Passing Along What I Learned

The Davis Center remembered me many years after graduation and I had the honor to be the commencement speaker at two career centers in the Fairfax County Public School system and I also shared my story with teachers, administrators, and school officials during their summer professional training.

people take time to get to know those with disabilities. It would have been easy for Booz Allen Hamilton to just let me finish my internship and go home. But they paid attention. They saw my skills. And they asked me to apply for the job as a clerk. I was hired for my skills, not because I have a disability. They had high expectations for me, and that made a big difference. My family had and still has high expectations as well. Both of my parents and the rest of my family believed in my abilities and have given me every opportunity to discover my unique talents and abilities.

My mom said it well when we traveled to Canada for the World Down Syndrome Congress in Vancouver in August 2006. While there, we were interviewed by Pamela Fayerman of the *Vancouver Sun*. The title of her front-page story was "All Children Do Well at Some Things and Not Others: Son's Ability 'Amazes' Mom." My mom told Pamela, "My child taught me more than I could ever imagine."[14]

No one could have imagined what I have become. But no one can imagine what anyone else is going to become either. That's why inclusion is so important. Giving everyone the same chances to learn makes a difference in how much they learn. And showing how different people can live, play, and work together is something

No Driver's License for Me

One possibility that never happened for me was learning to drive a car. I learned the rules of the road in my driver education elective, but my peripheral vision is poor. It's hard to be safe when driving if you can't see what's happening at the edges of your vision. So that was scratched off my list of things to accomplish. It's a good thing ride-sharing has come along. Maybe a self-driving car is in my future? Who knows?

that can start when children are little. It needs to be part of every student's school life.

Imagine how our world would be if everyone took the time to see people for who they are instead of who they seem to be. Some teachers didn't take time to look past my diagnosis of Down syndrome. They didn't see—or didn't want to see—that I had abilities they could have helped along. People like that are everywhere, not just educators. And think about teachers like Ms. Zola, who looked at me as a person with strengths to be encouraged and needs to be worked on.

IMAGINING NEW POSSIBILITIES

Everyone has abilities to be discovered and the possibility of putting them to work. My life has shown that to be true. I've learned from some people, and I've taught some things to others. People with intellectual disabilities are capable. I will share examples from projects in 2011 and 2012.

In 2011, we, people with Down syndrome, led an effort to teach others about what we could do. My friend, Karen Gaffney, and I planned this project for a year. It was a day-long event in Philadelphia that featured four people with Down syndrome with different talents.

Karen and her father presented on inclusive education and what it took for Karen to earn an associates of science degree at a community college in Oregon. (Karen is also a legend for her accomplishments in open-water swimming. She is the one who swam across the English Channel, a famously difficult feat. She also swam the width of Lake Tahoe.)

Sujeet Desai plays violin and other instruments beautifully, so he and his mother presented on music. Brad Hennefer is an excellent golfer, and he and his father talked about how everyone can learn to play golf. My mom and I talked about competitive employment and what I did to get my job at Booz Allen Hamilton's distribution center.

My presentation made an impression on Karen, who took away ideas for new possibilities for herself. In an e-mail, she wrote,

> While we were working on this conference, I learned a lot about what David did at his job, and then I learned even more when he prepared his materials for the workshop he did with his Mom. We also had a lot of time to talk leading up to the conference and at our celebration dinner after the conference! I came home from the event and told my Dad that I would really like to get a job in a "real company" like David.

So, I learned from David, and now, I have a good-paying job where I work about twenty-five hours a week, in addition to the work that I do with my own nonprofit organization![15]

On another occasion, in 2012, I helped a mother see the possibilities in her own son with Down syndrome and other people with Down syndrome throughout the world. I met Nicki Pombier Berger six months after her second son, Jonah, was born with Down syndrome. Nicki and I have a lot in common. We were born at the same hospital, just a year apart. And like my parents, she was working on graduate studies when she had a baby with Down syndrome. Just as my mom did when I was born, Nicki wanted to meet adults with Down syndrome. Staff at the National Down Syndrome Society referred her to me. Nicki came to visit me in Vienna, and we sat down to talk. This is how Nicki told the story:

> In one of our conversations that first day, David challenged me to think harder about what my role, as an oral historian working on this thesis, could be. "If you're not part of a larger conversation," he said, "you can talk and talk and talk, but nothing is going to get done. Yes, self-advocates like to talk a lot, they like to be behind the microphone. But what is it like for a self-advocate to be a board member for an organization? Or to be a valuable asset or resource to any organization? You can do all the stories you want," David told me, "but we want to do more."
>
> I wanted my thesis to be an opportunity for self-advocates to do more. I wanted to actualize the disability rights movement slogan of "nothing about us without us." I did not want to make stories "about" self-advocates, but wanted self-advocates, as David said, to be a real, valuable, powerful "resource" in the process of constructing this thesis project. So I asked David if he might want to work with me, to help me define how the project could really, in his words, do more. From that moment on, David was a major influence in shaping the project at the core of my graduate thesis. Most importantly, David helped me see the importance, to him and other self-advocates, of speaking beyond the disability community to audiences that might not hear them otherwise. Consequently, my oral history interviewing project took shape as an online collection of edited excerpts from the interviews, housed on Cowbird, a storytelling website with a large audience of the general public.
>
> One of the most memorable moments for me, in working with David on this project, was when we went back to our shared birthplace of Madison, Wisconsin, to present this work at the Oral History Association annual meeting in 2014. In that presentation, David implored my colleagues to include people with disabilities in our work, speaking

movingly about the importance of working with—not about—people with disabilities to tell a different story, a story about what is possible. David himself, standing there in command of the room, was a testament to the power of inclusion, and it is unthinkable to me to imagine what my education in "Down syndrome" might have been like, had I not learned through my relationships and conversations with David and the whole Egan family. I am forever grateful to David for opening his story to me, for working with me to tell stories with other self-advocates, and for changing the shape of my own story.[16]

Here's what I think: Your possibilities and the possibilities for people around you make up the possibilities for our community. It's like math, adding it all together to make one big, beautiful mountain of possibilities that can become real. If you can imagine that, maybe you can get other people to imagine it, too.

3

BECOMING A CHAMPION

David keeps you on your toes. He's full of surprises. I didn't
know David when he was younger, but I'm certain this has
always been the case. Looking back on the decade or so
we've now known one another, I'd say David has surprised
me most in the ways he's challenged me. He's challenged
my preconceptions, my compassion, and, even at times, my
physical ability.

—Travis Fulk, brother-in-law[1]

I was soaking wet, aching from the exhaustion of swimming a hard race,
and I was happy as can be. I had just climbed out of the pool where I
had beaten an older rival by a good margin, and I was walking back to my
team and coach.

There by the poolside was my mother. And there was the director of
the competition. They were talking. As I got closer, I could tell they were
disagreeing. And as I walked up and stood next to my mom, I thought
maybe they were even arguing. When I heard what they were discussing,
I couldn't help but smile.

I'll tell you about that in a moment, but first, let me say this: I love
sports. I love competing. I love winning. And I have become fond of the
color gold, the color of metal you see on many of the medals I have hanging in my bedroom at home.

When you're a kid, winning is one of the most important things, and
losing hurts more than you can bear sometimes. Now that I'm older, I
understand that winning isn't the most important thing about sports. The
friendships you make, the fitness you develop, the discipline you practice,
and the sense of fair play you learn are all wrapped up in sports. As a person

with Down syndrome, I learned there's even more involved than there is for a typical child. It's not just that nature puts challenges in the way, both physically and mentally. There's a entirely different side to it that my life in sports has made clear. And it's about expectations of what it takes—and what it means—to be a champion.

Back to the pool now.

A CONTESTED RACE

My mom was talking to Rick Jeffrey, whose job on that summer weekend was to make sure the competitions at the Special Olympics Virginia State Summer Games were run fairly. Special Olympics offers many sports for people who have intellectual disabilities. As in any big group of people, the athletes cover a wide range in terms of experience and ability. Part of the beauty of Special Olympics is how it arranges competitions to make each race, game, and match as fair, fun, and exciting as possible. Divisioning, as it is called, seems like a simple thing, simply grouping athletes up by age and ability into heats or teams of roughly the same competitiveness. In practice, it's very hard, and it is especially hard when you have people who are strong at a particular sport. Rick's role was guided by Special Olympics rules that spelled out what was allowed and what wasn't. And my mom was spelling out to Rick why, in this case, she thought the rules were wrong.

Here's what happened: I had qualified for the individual medley race with a very fast time. Only one other person had qualified with a time even close to mine. I was eleven years old, the product of neighborhood swim teams and very good coaches. My opponent was between fifteen and twenty years older than me. I was short, he was tall. Rick Jeffrey admitted later that the two of us standing there looked like a bad mismatch. It wasn't in the spirit of divisioning, to be honest, but it was allowed because how else were we two swimmers going to have a good race?

It was a good race. I won. I climbed out, happy with victory.

Meanwhile, my mom was having a lively discussion with Rick. Her point was simple: How can you expect a short eleven-year-old to not be intimidated by racing an adult who towers over him? Mom's background in psychology prepared her to make that case. All Rick could do was agree that it looked bad but was allowed by the rules so that two top-tier swimmers could have a meaningful race.

Rick told us his memories of that day in an e-mail. It read as follows:

By now Kathleen Egan is getting pretty worked up and raising her voice. It was pretty clear to me that she was hollering at me. She contends that it was just very noisy in the swim venue, and she was just making sure that I heard her. So in an effort to stall for a little time and gain some additional data, I asked Stann Bailey, the competition director, what the outcome of the race was. Who had won?

Stann Bailey: "Oh, David won by quite a nice margin."

I thought at this point that Kathleen Egan might be right; it was very noisy in the swim venue, and I had not heard Stann correctly. I repeated my question.

Stann Bailey: "David won easily."

It was at this point I look over at David, standing beside his mom, and notice the very big grin on his face. Never let it be said that a person with Down syndrome does not have a sense of humor. David has not only a good sense of humor, as I came to know, but he quickly realized that I did not have a lot of good answers for this argument and was now confused because we were not arguing outcomes but philosophy. . . . He was enjoying it.

Me (to both Stann and Kathleen): "Well, then what in the heck are we arguing about?"

Kathleen: "We are arguing about what's right. I know David won the race, but that does not mean that he did not feel intimidated. Plus, next time it might not be someone as confident as David but another athlete whose performance would be affected because of intimidation. Also, I am most concerned about the grown adult's viewpoint of having to swim against a younger kid. I know that the rules allow you to combine, but at some point it just looks bad, bad optics all around. This image of a little kid and grown man competing against each other is not what you want to use to create awareness about Special Olympics and all of the good outcomes this organization produces. We want Special Olympics to look the best it can because we believe in its mission."

Rick went on:

David and Kathleen and I have laughed about this memorable first encounter on many occasions. I imagine the look of incredulity on my face when I was given the information that David had actually won the race; well, I imagine that look on my face is what David really enjoyed that day.[2]

Rick Jeffrey was right. I did enjoy that moment, for a lot of reasons. When I think about it now, I remember it as a day when I won a race that my mom felt was unfair to both me and my competitor. It made me think a lot, for sure. Here's where fairness in sport comes into the picture, regardless of who won. My mom stood up for me, but she also stood up for the big man who I beat. She was my champion, and she was his champion.

BEING A CHAMPION

I know that being a *champion* can mean a few things, and winning is only part of being a champion. But *being someone's champion* means only one thing: advocating for someone, standing up for them, defending them. In my life, I've spoken up for others and myself. My parents made that a part of my upbringing, as you'll see in other chapters. It's hard to become a champion for others if people have not done the same for you. In school, Special Olympics, and the community, I've had kind, thoughtful people stand up and intercede in ways that helped me without helping them in any way. I want to tell you about champions on the playing field, both the ones who triumph and the ones who take up a cause on someone else's behalf.

My life in sports began when I was little. A ball was the first thing I loved enough to attempt to reach, stretch, and crawl to get. Now, at forty-two, I think I've played with almost every kind of ball there is. I've hit and caught baseballs and softballs. I've kicked, passed, and captured soccer balls. My hands know the weight and bounce of basketballs. And I have a good feel for the solid little balls I roll in bocce. I've bowled, I've played volleyball, I've played tennis. I've played the odd game of touch football.

But it is water that drew me to my first and greatest love, swimming.

Early on I was terrified of having my head under the water. I was introduced to the water as a passenger in a sailboat on Lake Mendota in Madison, Wisconsin. While my parents were graduate students at the University of Wisconsin, our neighbor, Professor Montoye, would sail with us on the lake in the summer. I vividly remember the sailboat swaying in the crisp, windy air on a sunny, blue-sky afternoon. I would watch as the sun would pierce and reflect off the tips of small waves. Getting my "sea legs" took a good deal of time. I had to be persuaded to overcome my initial hesitations in this wet and wobbly environment. My younger sister Teresa loved the water and would jump in when she was only eighteen months old. I loved imitating her, but even with sibling peer pressure, I was more cautious. Swimming became fun only when we moved to Falls Church, Virginia, and I was in a class with other kids.

When I saw my friend Pedro having a good time in the water, I began to turn into a "fish" myself. I was eight years old. My parents have told me that mimicking others has always been one of the ways I learned, developed, and grew. Obviously, mimicking has its pros and cons—you want to have good role models. I was lucky to have plenty of them. Pedro was my buddy and a great person to take after on those wonderful sunny days at the High Point Pool. If Pedro jumped into the water, I would also jump. Little by little, I lost the fear of having water in my eyes and learned to enjoy the splashing and games with Teresa and our friends.

I was ten when we moved to Vienna, Virginia, after hearing the schools would be a better fit for me. It was 1987. That year would be a big year for me in sports. I would practice and race as part of my local neighborhood swim team. I played baseball with the Vienna Little League. And it's the year I was introduced to track and field events with Special Olympics.

A Natural Love of Togetherness

I don't know if Pedro thought we were different, but either way it did not matter. We played, talked, and learned. Our innocence and love of the water was what we had in common. That and our love of being together. We were both little fellows, and we hadn't learned to be wary of differences.

It is only later in life that people learn to get hung up on differences and develop inhibitions about meeting new people. As my brother Marc would say, my intellectual and development disability does not need "two beers and a song you know" to loosen up at a party and have a good time. It's all natural.

MAKING THE TEAM

After we moved to Vienna, we joined the neighborhood swimming pool, Vienna Woods. The pool had great swim teams, and its swimmers often took top honors in Division 1 Northern Virginia Swimming League competitions.

The Vienna Woods swimming organization took swimming seriously. They had an A team made up of their best swimmers and a B team of swimmers who did not yet have the strength, skill, and experience to be top swimmers. They had an old-school approach: You earned your way onto the team, you put everything you had into practice and every race, and if you earned a trophy you got a trophy. If you didn't—well, there was always next year. And that means that I had to earn *my* place on the team, with no extra points for having an extra chromosome. So, I took swim classes to improve my strokes, form, and speed, and I earned my spot on the B team.

I made lots of friends, and it became second nature to be in the water. I was fully included in the relays and individual medley competitions. Swimming made me stronger and taught me discipline. I learned what it means to be part of a team and have others rely on me. Being challenged to improve and being a team, something bigger than myself, shaped my impressionable mind and views. I improved my technique in freestyle and butterfly, and I got faster and faster. We had good coaches who taught us the fundamentals. They wanted each swimmer to improve and excel at their favorite strokes.

I had similar experiences of belonging and seeing how champions are made when I played Little League baseball. I started in Falls Church and joined another team when we moved to Vienna. Again, I am drawn to people, so wanting to be part of the group is natural, no matter the activity. And it was on a sunny afternoon on the ball field where I got one of my first lessons in what it means to be a champion for others. And in this case, my teammates were champions for me.

We were huddled in the dugout on that hot spring afternoon. We were ten-year-olds enjoying being together and playing as a team. Practice was a little late to get started. That bugged me a little because I thrived on routine and repetition. I remember sitting there in the dugout wondering if someone had done something wrong. Were we in trouble? We were a motley crew of sorts. I had Down syndrome, and another player was missing his right arm. But we were pretty good, nowhere near as "bad" as the "Bad News Bears."

I had known a few of the boys on my baseball team from school and Cub Scouts, but of course I was in special-needs classes. We would see one another only at lunch, on the playground, at school assemblies, or at after-school activities. I did not fully understand the differences between myself and the other boys on my team, although I knew there were differences. I played hard and practiced hard, just as I did on the swim team. I felt I had earned my place on the baseball team. I was only ten, but no disability was going to get in the way of my competitive spirit. Thus, it was devastating when the coach's son turned to me and spoke.

"You cannot play on the team," he said.

I sat there in silence. I was stunned, trying to figure out what he meant.

"My dad wants us to win the town of Vienna's Little League championship for our division," the boy said. "We can't win with you on our team."

And then he told me I did not belong.

I was sad and perplexed. Would I be able to stay on the team?

These boys were my friends. I came to all the practices on time, and all I wanted was to play ball and have fun. I had a solid swing at bat. I ran the bases, making a few home runs from the errors common in Little League ball. I did all of the drills, and I paid attention to the coach's instructions. I was kind to my teammates and had a good attitude. It's true I was smaller than the other boys. They were quicker and nimbler. But I loved the game as much as, if not more than, the others. I was proud to be on the team, and I took the honor of being on the team seriously. I looked forward to the afternoon practices, the Saturday games, and giggling and chatting with friends. I just wanted to play ball.

What would happen now? My dad was sitting nearby, and he heard what was going on. He didn't have a chance to say or do anything before something truly wonderful happened.

One of my teammates, the best player on the team, said, "No! David plays on our team."

Other kids joined and also said, "We want David on the team."

The boys were adamant. "We will not play without David."

I've thought about that so many times. What was at stake? A championship.

And what did my teammates become? Champions—but champions for me.

I didn't have to defend myself. I didn't have to turn to my parents to protect me or speak up for me. The kids on the team did it. One leader had the courage to defend his teammate, and the others stood up for me, too. I don't think they thought about winning or losing a big game. I was part of their community of friends. I belonged with them. I was in their hearts.

And that was that. I proudly put on my glove and was ready to play ball.

And there were many games, many strikes, many outs, and, of course, many errors—but also lots of hard work, camaraderie, and good times. We came in second at the championship. Not too shabby for a team that on the surface seemed "imperfect." I think I may have helped in some way to help the team work together. A boy with Down syndrome and a player with one arm may have been a source of inspiration and motivation to try as hard as we did. We all gave a lot, and each one of us left it all—our sweat, our plays, our mistakes, our home runs—on the field.

WHAT I LEARNED FROM SPORTS

Being on the swimming and Little League baseball teams built a great foundation for me to grow both on and off the sports stage. Both built my confidence by giving me a way to shine. It was based on what I did by myself and for myself. Mom, Dad, and my siblings had given me a sense that I could do many things. But in the pool, it was just me swimming. I either did or didn't do well based on my skills and hunger to win. It was the same on the baseball field. No one from my family was going to hit, catch, or throw the ball for me. That really made it clear that there were things that I alone had to do. And I did well. In a lot of ways, I did more than I thought I could. Nothing builds confidence like that.

I grew in body and mind. Running, batting, throwing, and swimming built my big muscles. Gripping the baseball so I could throw it where it needed to go built my small muscles. Coordinating it all built balance, technique, and skill. At the same time, I learned to focus on key action amid the noise and activity on the baseball field. I learned the fine timing needed to launch myself into the pool when the race started. I kept track of my swimming opponents and baserunners using peripheral vision. And I learned the traditions of fair play and how to follow the many fine points of sport rules even though to this day, I still like to challenge the rules. It's just part of who I am.

It's worth mentioning that those early experiences and successes were possible because my physical development was not far behind the development of most boys my age. As kids with Down syndrome get older, the gap in development between them and most other boys gets wider. I stayed fit and strong by playing many sports, but Down syndrome put a wider and wider gap between me and others my age as I got older. The intellectual disability is only part of what sets people with Down syndrome apart. That third copy of the twenty-first chromosome affects every cell in my body, including my tendons and muscles. My legs and arms are shorter than most people's. Down syndrome hampers my coordination and slows my response times, too.

That explains a little bit about why a teammate would question how much I contributed to a Little League baseball team. A ten-year-old boy might be forgiven for blurting out what he may have heard others saying. Part of life is learning about the world and how things fit together. The teammates who rallied around me might not have been able to give a name to what they were doing, but I think it was something they learned during the course of the season. They met me on the first day of practice; learned my name was David; and saw me hit, run, throw, and catch. That made me a baseball player. They saw me working hard during each practice, just as they did. We became a team of friends with a wide range of abilities. For every star hitter, there were many others who struggled with batting. There was a boy who could naturally catch everything that came his way, and then there were the rest of us, who worked on skills and got better with practice. I fit right in, Down syndrome and all.

DISCOVERING A PLACE WHERE I COULD EXCEL

I didn't know it when I was ten, but my career in neighborhood sports was nearing its end because the other boys were getting so much stronger, faster, and bigger than me. It was in 1987, that my physical education teacher at my elementary school introduced me to sports with Special Olympics.

I started with track events, running as fast as I could against other people who also had intellectual and developmental disabilities. Suddenly, it was an entirely new playing field with an organization that understands how important sport and competition are for everyone. I embraced it with joy, crossing the finish line with my hands high in the sky. I had a big smile on my face when I won my first blue ribbon.

I stayed involved with community swimming and baseball for a while, but eventually Special Olympics became my sports world. The coaches in Special Olympics came to practices with patience, devotion, and an openness to working with people at every skill level. That helped me set goals I could achieve, and that built my self-confidence and self-reliance.

I think Special Olympics is the greatest stage in the world because of its amazing fans, volunteers, and friends. It triggered the champion in me and helped me feel respected for who I am. I had a sport for each season of the year, so I was also training and competing. I took part in track and field, swimming, speed skating, tennis, table tennis, basketball, softball, soccer, and bocce.

I am glad my parents got me involved in neighborhood sports first. They strengthened my skills and built my love of sports and competition. They gave me the advantage of learning to work hard and play hard. I easily learned new sports and gained new skills. But Special Olympics was different when I needed a safe and honest space to acknowledge my disability, move forward, and not feel alone anymore. Earlier in my life, I had been surrounded by children who didn't struggle with physical skills the way I did. In Special Olympics, I realized I was not the only one who had adversity and a disability from day one.

Special Olympics changed my life and that of my entire family. It's a worldwide organization that focuses on making champions on the playing field and building the confidence in people to be champions for themselves and others. Special Olympics has been such a big influence in my life in so many ways. I talk about many of those ways in other chapters, but here, it's all about sports.

My family got involved with Special Olympics, too. My dad and younger brother Marc have been coaches. My sisters helped me with my speed skating. My mom helped in every way possible, including teaching me the fine art of dribbling a basketball when I was small. The Special Olympics approach to competition influenced us all as we celebrated small and big improvements, beating one's own records in swimming and speed skating to learning to be a selfless player in team sports. Here are some memorable moments along my path to becoming a champion in Special Olympics sports.

IN THE POOL

In swimming, I had two exceptional coaches. Ginny Theisen tuned in to each swimmer's unique talents and knew how to motivate us to swim faster and better. Parker Ramsdell was a great swimmer who volunteered to coach me during his middle school and high school years. They both took me seriously and treated me as a swimmer rather than someone with a disability who swam. They saw my skill and potential, and they worked me hard. I improved tremendously with their guidance.

Parker and I became close friends. Before a big race at the 2003 Special Olympics Virginia Summer Games in Richmond, he sent me an encouraging e-mail.

> David, I can never express how proud of you I am. You always gave me a 100 percent effort at practice and always showed that *mental toughness* I talked about. When you are swimming your 100 free or 100 IM and start to feel a little bit of pain, remember those hard one hundred-yard sets that we did and how much those hurt and realize that the pain you felt at practice was to prepare you for this meet to make you a better swimmer. When the going gets tough, the tough get going. You are ready to whoop some butt.

Remember that your time is more important than your place, and your effort is more important than anything else. Give these races everything you've got. Richmond is waiting, now go down there and do your thing and bring your four *gold* medals to my party Saturday night.

He signed it, "Your coach, but more importantly your pal, Parker."[3]

I did not disappoint my friend. I came back with four gold medals, and, more importantly, I beat my own record. That made Parker smile. I'll share some more stories about how Parker and I came together later.

ON THE COURT

I love basketball, but at first, I didn't share the ball. I learned by doing everything myself, from dribbling to shooting. At home, we had all kinds of balls, and my mom taught me how to dribble at a young age. I would go with her to the community center where my sister Teresa did gymnastics. During her practices, my mom and I played ball. She taught me how to protect the ball and keep dribbling. Having my mom as my teacher is kind of amazing. She grew up in the old city of Jerusalem during turbulent times. When did she have time to become this dribbling wizard? In any case, she pushed me to learn the fundamentals of basketball.

I had all the fundamentals, but what I was missing was the team-player perspective. As I was playing basketball for Special Olympics in high school, I began to realize that I am shorter than many of the other athletes on the team. That means they had a better chance of scoring, so it was in my team's best interest for me to pass to them. It was hard at first. I wanted to be in charge of the court. It was a good lesson that team play was the way to victory. I stopped trying to keep the ball and dribble it for eternity. I also gave up my mostly

My Amazing Moves

In 2016, a film crew with Attitude Pictures came all the way from New Zealand to create a documentary about me called *What's Up with Down Syndrome*. They followed me for four days as I went to Capitol Hill, the National Institutes of Health, my job with CBRE, and my Saturday basketball games with Special Olympics. They featured my team and our amazing moves on and off the court. They captured our spirit and love for basketball. If you have a chance, you should watch it. You'll find it at attitudepictures.com and on my website: davideganadvocacy.com.

unsuccessful attempts to shoot while I was being guarded by much taller people. I used my agility and some of the moves I learned from watching the best point guards on TV. I became the hardworking point guard who made my teammates the heroes. In basketball, either the entire team wins or the entire team loses. If you want to be a champion, you need to help your entire team be champions, too. But I have to say, being short has its advantages when you have a sweet underhanded layup like I do.

UNIFIED ON THE SOFTBALL DIAMOND

One of the most amazing and inclusive things about Special Olympics is its Unified Sports. Unified Sports teams mix people both with and without intellectual disabilities. They play together against other Unified teams. It's simple, and it's brilliant.

Unified Sports is great in many ways. My first experience with this kind of thing was in basketball when coach Troy Villemaire was in charge. He invited excellent players in high school to play with us, and our teams became stronger as a result. Playing Unified with top-notch athletes motivated us to learn

The Thrill of Softball

I've been playing Unified softball for more than twelve years, and it is a blast. I was skeptical at first with my history as a baseball player. Softball is for girls, I thought, since that's the way it played out in high school. But it is great! I love playing catcher and getting to throw off the mask and stare down the baserunners.

new skills and gave us role models of good teamwork and cooperative play. We were not the only ones to benefit, however. The real goal of Unified Sports is to get people with different abilities and backgrounds to play together as teammates.

During my Little League days, most of the players naturally accepted me as part of the team. Unified Sports aims at an older crowd but has the same goal: making it easy for people with and without disabilities to get to know one another through the bonding power of team sports. For Special Olympics athletes who may feel isolated in their everyday lives, being teammates with Unified Sports partners can open the door to new friendships on and off the playing field.

For my family, it's been a great way for us to play sports together. My brother Marc got involved first and then got me to play on his team. He became the coach, and we recruited my brother-in-law, Travis, and

Marc's wife, Juline, to play on the team. Many of Marc's friends have joined in, one of whom was a friend who played Little League baseball with Marc.

The mix of players makes for an entirely new kind of Special Olympics experience. When Marc was a brand-new coach, he found out quickly how intense an experience it could be. Powerful hitters, both athletes and partners, forced him to make strategic changes on the run. It was a more competitive and exciting kind of play than he had expected. Marc finds his Unified Sports experience to be incredibly rewarding:

Mom at Bat

The rules of Unified Sports require an even balance of Special Olympics athletes and partners, and that led to a situation at a state tournament where he had to get creative. To avoid being disqualified, Marc coaxed my dad into taking his position as coach so Marc could play. The team still needed one more person. My mom, who had never held a bat in her seventy-three years, stood at the plate once per inning so that our team could play. She was everyone's champion on that hot day.

I ended up getting more out of it than even the athletes in certain respects. You come to see that the simplicity of life of just getting together with friends and joining in a challenging game to give your best is what matters most in life. It is not about being the best out there but being the best of yourself. It is a beautiful event to watch all different walks of life and people get behind a movement of wanting those with disabilities to excel. Not to mention it is incredibly refreshing being around people who do not have a malicious bone in their bodies. The athletes teach you patience for them and for yourself. They teach you that it is okay to just give your best—that's all we can ask for of ourselves. Knowing that someone is counting on you so deeply gives you a fulfilling sense of purpose that you cannot get anywhere else.[4]

A LIFE OF COMPETITION

If you ever go to a Special Olympics summer games, go to the track. The 100-meter dash is a pure and simple event: two or more people racing from the starting line to the finish line. There's only one way to win. There are many heats of the 100-meter, from fastest to slowest. Every boy or girl, man or woman wants to win. You can see it in every race, no matter how fast they run, that urge to be a champion in *this* race today, *right now*.

I am forty-two now, and I've been playing sports for more than three decades. Most of that time has been with Special Olympics. Throughout the years, I have competed in many different sports and won ribbons or medals. Each of them is meaningful. The idea that Special Olympics sports are easy and that everyone gets a medal is a myth. Quite a bit of time and thought goes into setting up matches and races so that the competitors are fairly matched, as I mentioned at the start of the chapter. The reason so much effort goes into it is because everyone wants to be a champion.

Who can say that anyone who wants to be a champion can't be one because of a disability? Special Olympics understands the basic human need to show what you can do and be part of an organization built on respect.

Champions are not only the people with famous names and big salaries. At every level of competition, from Little League baseball to Unified Sports, I've felt the impact of victories and losses. I compete because feeling like a champion is one of the best feelings in the world. Being on a team that has just won a championship is even better because you share it with people you've learned to love and trust through hard work and countless practices.

By my family's involvement with Special Olympics at the local, state, and international levels, we have all become champions in one way or another. It continues to be a path that we embrace and continue to love as it has evolved throughout the years into helping not only the individual athlete, but also the families and society at large to see us as valuable human beings.

My Trophy Display

I proudly showcase my more than three hundred medals and ribbons in a wooden trophy display in my bedroom. The trophy display means a lot to me because it was made by "Papa Eugene," who was like a grandfather to me. He was a Canadian Franciscan brother and a carpenter/wood carver. Papa Eugene knew my mother as a little girl in the old city of Jerusalem a long time ago and became a surrogate father, as her dad passed away when she only was five years old. Many people who visit us have also admired the trophy display furniture.

RETHINKING "ABILITY"

One of the many visitors to our house throughout the years was Dr. Sujata Bardhan. I gave her a tour of the house, and no tour is complete without visiting my room, where I keep my medals and ribbons. Dr. Bardhan was impressed. She wrote this to me:

> What I remember the most of my visit was when I entered David's room. I had no idea that I was going to be in awe of his achievements forever. I was simply blown away by the amount of shiny trophies, medals, and certificates that were beautifully displayed in his room, proof of his achievements as an athlete in Special Olympics, proof of what anyone can do with or without a disability. I remember thinking whether this was a different ability and not just a label we call disability. I remember taking a picture of the medals so that I could show it to my children as inspiration of someone who had achieved so much with odds stacked against them. During this visit, I realized that anything was possible if one had the means, the determination, and the support of a family that can push oneself to achieve their best. David Egan, the person with an extra chromosome, taught me that the sky can be the limit, and he was not defined by a label![5]

4

OPENING DOORS

> David was born a leader. Born to inspire everyone around
> him. He has the confidence to walk into the CEOs office any
> time and say, "Mary, I want to talk to you and share my opin-
> ion." He never feels like he needs to make an appointment. I
> am proud that he has the confidence to do that! He has a real
> grasp of the importance of progressing in his life and using the
> skills he has acquired to achieve great things.
>
> —Mary Davis, CEO of Special Olympics Inc.[1]

People often ask me, "When did you start your advocacy?" There is no
specific time, place, or event that launched my advocacy efforts. I believe deep down that I was born to be an advocate, and things happened in
my life that propelled me to do this good work. When I was in preschool
and kindergarten, I was just one of many boys and girls in the classrooms,
fully part of what went on. So I learned to speak up for myself. That was
just as important to my growth as an advocate as being chosen as an adult
to speak in front of thousands of people.

Those two phases of my life were years apart. Throughout the years,
there were opportunities that little by little helped me evolve into an eager
and active advocate. Being an advocate for yourself or others means breaking through some barrier to get at something important. I have done that
all my life, and I intend to continue unlocking doors through advocacy in
the future. I proudly consider myself a trailblazer.

A trailblazer is someone who makes his own path where there was
no path before. The "blaze" that a trailblazer leaves behind is not a fire,
but a mark left for others to follow. I did that, too, but I wasn't out in the
wilderness by myself. As you will see, some unexpected events created op-

portunities, and with each opportunity, there was someone who helped. When those doors opened, I went through and found myself in a new place with still more opportunities to come. It's my nature to look for new things to do. That's one of the reasons I was featured in a book called *Firestarters* in 2018[2] (again, not real fires!). The authors called me an "instigator," someone who "disrupts things"[3] and creates and initiates new beginnings. I hadn't thought about myself in that way, but when they wrote it, it really made sense to me.

My advocacy grew bit by bit, as I said, until 1999. That's when an unexpected opportunity opened my eyes to the thrill and satisfaction of speaking on behalf of others. And what's funny about this is that the opportunity came about after a big disappointment. And when I say big disappointment, I mean a crushing one.

MY SHOT AT SWIMMING IN
THE SPECIAL OLYMPICS WORLD GAMES

In 1999, Special Olympics held its World Summer Games in North Carolina. I live in Virginia, just a few hours by car from the cities where the games would be held: Raleigh-Durham and Chapel Hill. I was a champion swimmer then. My dream was to compete in a Special Olympics World Games, and I thought 1999 was my year. I had been winning gold medals in Special Olympics Virginia games for years, so I was sure I would be chosen to represent Virginia at the games in North Carolina.

I am a good swimmer. When I was on my local pool's swim team, I raced against swimmers from throughout the area. I was the only one with Down syndrome, so I had to work hard and swim well to compete successfully. That training and experience paid off when I started swimming for Special Olympics. After all of that, in 1999, I was twenty-two years old, fit, and well-prepared to compete. I could feel in my veins the desire to win. My friend and volunteer swimming coach, Parker Ramsdell, had prepared me well. In a way, Parker opened a door to me to a new way of looking at swimming as a sport of power, technique, style, and rhythm.

MY YOUNG COACH

I had met Parker by chance at Oak Marr Recreation Center, a county-run pool close to my home where Special Olympics trained athletes in adaptive swimming. At the time we met, he was young, just in middle school, but already he was a remarkable competitive swimmer. The Oak Marr center is huge, with a deep diving well, two wide sections of swimming lanes, and a big area called a beach, which is sloped underwater so kids and others can play in water of varying depths. Somehow, in that big place, Parker noticed me swimming in the pool during my practices and saw I had the potential to do better and become a faster swimmer. By that time, I had been swimming for years, and I thought I knew my stuff. But Parker would bring a new level of performance to my swimming. He graduated from Madison High School in 2003. At Madison High he had helped his swimming team earn district titles in 2001 and 2002. He is acknowledged in our neighborhood of Oakton and Vienna as a great swimming coach.[4]

Parker asked his mom if he could work with me as a volunteer coach. His mom spoke with my mom, and they agreed I could train with Parker once a week, in addition to the Special Olympics practices. As soon as we started, I noticed the first big difference: My previous coaches had given instruction from the side of the pool. Parker jumped in the water and gave me every lesson in the pool. It was amazing. And it really worked.

That was the start of many great years of training and friendship. (Parker went on to become a well-respected trainer at Oak Marr with the York Swim Club of Northern Virginia. Many young swimmers are still benefitting from his amazing coaching abilities.)

> **Meeting High Expectations**
>
> Parker understood inclusion well. He did not give me any slack because I was in Special Olympics. He saw potential, assumed I was capable, and expected me to be the best swimmer I could be. While Parker went to college at the University of Austin, Texas, he got in touch when he would visit his family for the holidays. We would go out and catch up. After various different career paths, Parker is still involved with Special Olympics and still my friend. We need more Parkers in this world.

What really made a difference is that Parker took me seriously. He assumed I could understand his directions and learn and improve. He took on every aspect of my approach—strokes, breathing, kicks, posture—and helped me become a great swimmer. He taught me how to trim seconds off my times by using flip turns.

His coaching paid off. I had qualified to swim at the Special Olympics Virginia games every summer for years but now was stronger than before. In 1999, he had been coaching me for two years, and I was the fastest I had ever been. It was gold, gold, gold, gold in each of my four races. We both thought there was no chance I'd be passed over for the World Games.

TURNING DISAPPOINTMENT INTO OPPORTUNITY

What we did not know is that winning gold medals is not the only standard for selection for Special Olympics World Games. Every sport in Special Olympics has divisions based on age and ability. It's one of the things that keeps Special Olympics competitions fair and exciting for athletes. Since their abilities span a wide range, it wouldn't be fair for the fastest athletes to race against the slowest athletes. Instead, athletes compete against others who are at about the same competitive level. Each set of ability-based divisions has its own set of medals. Thus, the fastest swimmer in a group of slow swimmers could win a gold medal. And the fastest swimmer in a group of fast swimmers could also win a gold medal. That was me, winning gold in Division 1, the fastest group of swimmers.

There's a tricky part, however. Athletes in every division, from slowest to fastest, have a shot at going to the World Games. The team for the World Games is small and chosen by lottery. After all my preparation, all my winning, and all my hopes, the final choice was left to random chance. And I was not among the lucky few. At first, I was truly devastated by the outcome. I was sad and felt defeated. I felt angry, too.

But a trailblazer can't give up. It's not in his nature, and it's not in mine. So I looked for a different path, and I found it, volunteering at the Special Olympics 1999 World Summer Games. It was my chance to give back to an organization that had given so much to me. Volunteering was my opportunity to travel to North Carolina, participate in the many varied events, and celebrate with other athletes.

I see myself in the other athletes, and it is as if I am competing along with them. I know how they feel. I know what it is to train all year, get ready for a big event, and ultimately give it your best. Plus, I love a challenge.

The theme of the 1999 Games was, "It's all about attitude." I believe that whether you are an athlete, coach, or volunteer, everyone is a star at the World Games. I was committed to contributing in any way I could. If I couldn't swim, I could help out behind the scenes. Well, that was the plan.

"I'M AN ATHLETE"

The World Games were held from June 26 to July 4, and seven thousand athletes from one hundred fifty countries competed in nineteen sports. Superstar musician Stevie Wonder was there. Former Olympic swimmer Donna de Varona and the Olympic gymnast Bart Conner were there, too. Famous evangelical minister Billy Graham and many other celebrities were there. It was a big event, and I was proud and excited to be there.

We stayed with my Aunt Pat and Uncle Ron Wharton. As locals, they had helped host the athletes from Special Olympics Bermuda the week before. They were excited about the Games and delighted to have us staying with them.

My mother volunteered as an interpreter. I was given the job of escorting members of the media. It was the perfect assignment for me because I loved watching the news on TV and cable. It was great to meet journalists and play a small part in helping them produce stories about the Games. And that is where a door unexpectedly opened after my swimming dream went down with a soggy splash.

The media crew I was with was eager to interview and film a Special Olympics athlete. It was not always easy to coordinate schedules and get approvals. They were getting frustrated. I wanted to help them, and to me there was an easy and obvious solution to the problem.

"I am an athlete," I told the crew. We talked for a little while. They decided to interview me and get film of me swimming. And that means I got to swim at the World Games after all. Just not for competition.[5] The next day I was on WRAL 5, a local TV news station in Raleigh. That unexpected opportunity quickly turned into taking part in a Special Olympics press event the following day. The man in charge of Special Olympics programs for athletes to become leaders and public speakers was Dave Lenox. After he saw what I did without preparation in North Carolina, he made sure I was involved in other athlete leadership events. He wrote,

> I first met David Egan at the 1999 World Summer Special Olympics Games in Raleigh, NC. There was a *lot* going on as delegations arrived. When that happens, it is easy to let subtleties slip and to miss opportunities. David was the perfect person in the perfect place. While we were scurrying around, David stopped to ask who was talking to a

particular sponsor. He offered to meet the sponsor for us. He brought a very personal touch and message at a time when others would have been overly rushed and transactional. What I think a lot of people miss is the confidence and sense of purpose that it took for David to step into that role. He didn't hesitate to volunteer because he *knew* that he knew Special Olympics and its power better than anyone else in the room. That is what being a leader is all about. He used a realistic self-assessment of his own skills to guide his action and make a difference. I have seen David do this repeatedly over the last twenty years. He has been able to step into roles that are substantive and impactful. Another athlete leader pointed out that David is able to listen as people asked questions and then answer them. He acknowledged that he couldn't do that: *I feel like I played a role in starting the conversation, but David advanced it.* When people hear about someone who has intellectual disabilities taking on leadership roles or high-profile positions, I think they frequently assume it is a token role or publicity stunt. When David Egan takes one of those roles, he changes the conversation to a more substantive one about clarity and purpose.[6]

A TURNING POINT

That was just the start of my acting as a spokesperson for Special Olympics and other organizations that promote human dignity, respect, and inclusion for everyone. People started to hear about me after the World Games in North Carolina, and the opportunities kept coming. I was interviewed for a Special Olympics magazine called *Spirit*, and what I said then is still true: "Special Olympics makes a difference in my life, and I hope it continues making a difference in the lives of many people all over the world."[7]

Many new doors opened for me to pursue public speaking and be an eager and active advocate. Throughout the years, I would speak at more than twelve events per year in not only my home state of Virginia, but also throughout the United States and internationally. There were years when I would be engaged more than twice a month, speaking for fundraisers, educators' professional meetings, various conferences, big and small business meetings, galas, races, and other events, spreading a message of hope and determination.

For example, in 2014, the Down Syndrome Family Network (DSFN) in Trinidad-Tobago asked me to visit their sunny home in the Caribbean to speak about employment. I spoke to not only their group, but also officials in the government, community businesses, and the local office of the U.S.

Agency for International Development. I was interviewed by TV stations about my life and points of view. It went really well. A few years later, in 2018, DSFN invited me back to speak again.

I also went to conferences where I was able to meet other advocates and learn from them. In addition, I had the chance to be part of the process of charting new approaches for the Special Olympics movement. I went from the swimming pool to the inner circle of decision makers, and it was great. The Special Olympics initiative that taught and coached athletes to become leaders is called the Athlete Leadership Program. Dave Lenox led the program, and I learned a lot from it. I also had exciting opportunities that I might never have experienced.

One of those opportunities was in April 2000. I had been selected as a delegate to the Special Olympics Global Athlete Congress in the Hague, Netherlands. The city is the seat of the Dutch parliament, also home to the UN's international Court of Justice and the International Criminal Court. Special Olympics athletes from every region of the world came together to discuss their visions for the future of Special Olympics. Despite differences in language and cultures, we held many discussions, reflected on the Special Olympics movement, and proposed new strategies.

The flight to the Netherlands was my first as a representative of the United States, and the event was the first Special Olympics Global Athlete Congress. I had traveled overseas as a child with my family, but this time it was different. I was flying on my own as part of a Special Olympics team.

My employer at the time was Booz Allen Hamilton, and it just so happened that the company had a strong partnership with Special Olympics, offering pro bono consultation on strategic planning. Booz Allen Hamilton was also a sponsor of the Global Athlete Congress

> **Mom Took Part**
>
> My mom also joined the event. She was in Thailand on a business trip at that time and had arranged to meet me in the Netherlands on her way back home. During the congress, there were family working groups, and she participated in those discussions. I was so glad she could contribute and see me in action.

in the Netherlands. My immediate supervisor was elated that I was among the Special Olympics athletes chosen to represent the United States at the congress. I told Isaac Webb, my distribution center manager, that I was going to give a speech there. He wanted me to shine. He asked Paul Berry,[8] a well-known and respected senior news anchor at the ABC-7 (WJLA-TV) station in Washington, DC, to give me some pointers. It was an honor to work with such an experienced speaker. We worked and had a few laughs as I was rehearsing with him.

Mr. Berry taught me to focus on the audience and get them to interact with me. He would say, "You are in charge of the stage. Grab their attention." Mr. Berry had a big heart. When he laughed or spoke, his voice resonated throughout the room. He grabbed the attention of his listeners. He was a great humanitarian and known to care about people. He cared about me and wanted me to succeed. We met a few times, and before I knew it I was ready to speak in the Netherlands.

THE CONGRESS IN THE NETHERLANDS

My speech was titled "Finding Yourself." It starts with accepting who you are and discovering that unique talent that makes you one of a kind. We all have it, but we may be unaware of our talents. "Find your spirit and follow it throughout life," I said.

I shared my journey and my pride in being employed by Booz Allen Hamilton. I spoke about how Special Olympics has changed my life. It has helped me as a person and an athlete to realize my dreams and touch other people's hearts.

The Global Athlete Congress had several purposes, and each was related. First, it gave athletes with intellectual disabilities a clear and direct voice in shaping the future of Special Olympics. Each athlete represented a country, but each also represented one of the world regions where Special Olympics operates. Having so many different points of view made for a lively and enlightening several days. Second, we were asked to make recommendations to improve Special Olympics. And since the event was promoted through press releases and press opportunities in the Netherlands, the world had a chance to see that Special Olympics treated us as true leaders. People everywhere could see that we are creative, capable, talented leaders with good ideas and many skills.

As athletes, one of the things we care about most is the sports we play. There were several topics to discuss, for example, the athlete and coach codes of conduct and the process for selecting athletes to attend the World Games. (I was very interested in that one.) More importantly, we asked that Special Olympics start using the term *intellectual disability* to describe us instead of the older term, *mental retardation.* (Special Olympics stopped using the old term soon thereafter.) We also urged Special Olympics leaders to work for more outreach in the community and with the media, and to encourage families to be more active and involved.

The 2000 Global Athlete Congress was a big boost for my confidence as a leader. I found out that I was not alone. Many others throughout the world with intellectual disabilities like me were as eager as I am to make changes in this world.

JOINING THE LEADERSHIP COUNCIL

When I got back from the Netherlands, Dave Lenox wrote to let me know I had been selected to join the United States Leadership Council in the Athlete Leadership Program Subcommittee. In his congratulations letter he wrote, "I am looking forward to your participation in our conference calls and in our meetings. Your ideas are always thought-provoking, and I am sure they will challenge us to do even greater work in 2001."[9]

I went to the training in Atlanta, followed by a memorable trip to Las Vegas with a few leaders to share ideas about how to sustain and promote leadership among athletes. In addition to the busy meetings with various representatives from different states in the United States, it was also a fun time in the evenings. I took a gondola at the Venetian and pretended to be in Italy. The casinos did not attract me much, but I enjoyed a circus show.

The next international Global Athlete Congress I attended was in 2010, in Morocco, under the patronage of his majesty King Mohamed VI and his sister, her Royal Highness Princess Lalla Amina. She led the Special Olympics strategic meetings in their country. They gave us a red-carpet welcome and treated us to royal settings under big tents in the city of Marrakesh. I traveled to that event with my mentor, David Thomason, and learned so much working with him.

I am very thankful to David Thomason and Dave Lenox for their work with the Athlete Leadership Program, because it gave me and others more opportunities to act as leaders. The goal of the program is to allow athletes to explore opportunities for greater participation in the Special Olympics movement beyond sports training and competition. The program gave athletes with intellectual disabilities the chance to act as coaches, referees, team captains, spokespeople, and board and committee members. These roles give athletes a voice in shaping the movement and a chance to spread the word about the transformations Special Olympics can bring to individuals and families. The Athlete Leadership Program also provides a way for athletes to showcase talents and interests that may have gone unnoticed. It is designed to create new avenues for the athletes to contribute. It gives us the tools to open doors and explore new opportunities.

A GLOBAL ROLE FOR ME AND OTHERS

The Athlete Leadership Program has trained and developed hundreds of athlete leaders throughout the world. There are different levels in the program. The highest level is to be a Sargent Shriver International Global Messenger. (Sargent Shriver was the husband of Special Olympics founder Eunice Kennedy Shriver. He founded the Peace Corps, among many other things. I met him when I was ten years old.)

I was honored and privileged to be chosen as an International Global Messenger (IGM) for four years, from 2014 to 2018. I was one of twelve people chosen from throughout the world. My fellow IGMs were from every part of the world. We spoke at local and international events. We learned from one another and became friends. It was amazing to have the opportunity to learn so much about the world and be a spokesman for Special Olympics.

One of the peak moments for me was standing in front of an audience of more than sixty thousand people at the opening ceremony for the 2015 Special Olympics World Summer Games in Los Angeles. I looked out on the audience of athletes, coaches, families, and the many thousands of people who came to join our enormous celebration. Los Angeles Memorial Coliseum was the site of the 1932 and 1984 Olympics, and hundreds of other important events. Being in that big, old place now so full of color and joy filled me with excitement. I was standing on the same stage as First Lady Michelle Obama, music superstar Stevie Wonder, NFL star Jamaal Charles, and other celebrities. I knew many more eyes were on me because the event was also being shown on ESPN.

I had a message and a hope, that the words I spoke would open unexpected doors in the lives of others, just as opportunities had opened doors for me. I don't know if people in the audience or watching on TV that night saw me and others with new understanding. But I think they did.

ADDING A NEW VOICE

The idea of being included in everyday life is important to me because it's so easy to be excluded when you have a disability. It's so much easier now to take part in all kinds of activities that might have not been available to a person with Down syndrome years ago. At the risk of repeating myself, many people with Down syndrome were kept out of the public eye in institutions from the day they were born. Our society in the United States is usually welcoming of me and others like me. There are always people who react unkindly to people with disabilities, but it's less common than ever, I feel.

I decided that I want to speak up for people with disabilities and help influence the decisions that are made about me and others like me. One way to do that, I thought, would be through taking a leadership role in organizations that advocate for people with Down syndrome. I started close to home. I wanted to join the board of directors of the Down Syndrome Association of Northern Virginia (DSANV). The board took the idea seriously and interviewed several candidates. It was new, an experiment in leadership. The board members knew having someone with Down syndrome would add a new perspective, but they wondered if a person with Down syndrome could follow and contribute to discussions about the finances and policies. Most board members at that time had young children with Down syndrome and were not familiar with adults like me. Eventually, the board agreed to pursue interviewing and selecting a person with Down syndrome to serve on their board. They chose me as their first board member with Down syndrome.

Lisa Roti was vice president at DSANV at that time, and we bonded quickly. Lisa and her husband Todd have two daughters, Grace and Hannah. Hannah has Down syndrome. Lisa wrote the following about my time on the board of directors:

> David was a great example to the other board members/parents. He always listened intently to the issues being discussed while we talked past each other. He would then come up with a unique idea and perspective that none of us had considered. His solutions were all rooted in the same premise, that the disability community needs to find common ground and work together to achieve our goals.
>
> David is a strong emissary and voice for those who have "other" abilities and cannot advocate for themselves. We are always impressed seeing him speak on his own educational experiences, involvement with Special Olympics, or the importance of employment. Audiences ranging from small parent groups to members of the United Nations are equally impressed and moved by his message. We always remember one of his most important lessons is that individuals with developmental disabilities don't want a job, they want a career![10]

Phil Pedlikin was president of DSANV, and he saw great value in having me on his team. He challenged me. We traveled together to various conferences. Together with Phil, Lisa, and Steve Beck, I was there around the kitchen table where the first discussions about the ABLE Act were held. Many of the meetings took place at DSANV members' homes, including mine. I loved those early years of DSANV and am so proud to have been on Capitol Hill when the ABLE Act was passed in Congress with a bipartisan vote.

> **About the ABLE Act**
>
> The Achieving a Better Life Experience (ABLE) Act of 2014 allows people with disabilities to save money tax-free so they can pay for some disability expenses. In most cases, the money in an ABLE account does not count as income, so it helps safeguard government benefits for people who receive them.[11]

My service on the board seems to have changed the minds of DSANV leaders. There are now three individuals with Down syndrome on that board. Having us on the Board of Directors allows us to add a dimension that had been missing, an insider's perspective on what it means to have Down syndrome. Every board member comes with particular interests and skills. Our skills are not necessarily related to strategic planning or budgeting, but we are motivating messengers for fundraising and giving hope to new parents of children with Down syndrome. It says a lot to a new parent that a person with Down syndrome can be a leader in the community. I am glad the DSANV board decided to take that chance.

After being on the board of DSANV, I had the opportunity to be a member of other boards of directors. I joined the board of Down Syndrome Affiliates in Action (DSAIA), a trade association for Down syndrome organizations throughout the United States. DSAIA, a nonprofit, represents dozens of organizations. One of my goals was to encourage the association to have a person with Down syndrome on the board of each organization in every state. Together with my mom, we did a survey and found that few DSAIA member organizations had a person with Down syndrome on their boards. Today many do.

I also got the chance to serve on the board of Special Olympics Virginia. During my three years on that board, my mentor, Beth Frank, took me seriously and helped me in many ways. We spent long hours at home preparing for board meetings and together would drive the one hundred miles to Richmond, where the meetings were held.

I asked Beth to help me make a motion to encourage Special Olympics Virginia to hire someone with an intellectual disability. She taught me how to approach the topic and, most importantly, gave me tips on securing votes from interested members ahead of meetings. Many members of the board and Special Olympics Virginia staff supported the idea, so it wasn't long before that hire was made.

OPENING DOORS FOR OTHERS

Every time I talk to people, whether in one-on-one situations or in big audiences, I hope that what I say changes something in them. One time I was working with my good friend and mentor, David Thomason, of Special Olympics Virginia, to get ready for a conference of Special Olympics supporters. We were working with Toastmasters International, the nonprofit organization that helps people improve their public speaking skills through practice in clubs throughout the world.

"With each meeting, it was clear that—while our athletes were getting more and more comfortable with their roles and feeling more prepared—our friends at Toastmasters were learning quite a bit as well," David wrote in an e-mail to me. "During these trainings, with each interaction, David and his fellow Global Messengers opened the minds of those around them."[12]

My friend David Thomason could tell something was going on, something he couldn't quite identify. And then he found out that one of the Toastmaster participants was pregnant. One of her tests showed there was a chance her baby had Down syndrome. David wrote,

> In a heartfelt, candid, and very transparent way, she shared that she had originally been uncertain about how she was going to deal with the news about her yet-to-be-born baby. Then, she said that though she had been unsure how to deal with this news, after working with and spending this time with David and his friends—any doubt about the capabilities, potential for fulfilling and rewarding lives, or other concern she had about those with Down syndrome—had dissolved. Thanks to her work with David, she unquestionably knew that—regardless of test results—she would proceed with her pregnancy, welcome and love her child unconditionally, and not let the fear of that unknown change her choices. That "unknown" was much less of an unknown now because of David's influence. Genuine interaction had allowed for a deeper, far more informed understanding. This moment of life-changing impact— for all involved—will stay with me forever.[13]

You never know when doors will open for you. You never know what new trails you will find when a path you think you are on suddenly comes to a dead end. And even if your path stays open, wide, and easy to travel, beautiful opportunities may show themselves as you turn a corner. My parents didn't know it when I was born, but I opened a door for them, too. I am so glad they were the kind of people, even as young as they were, to have faith in themselves and see the potential in me when almost everyone else around them seemed in favor of sending me off to an institution. That's the thing about doors, isn't it? You never know what's behind them unless you open them and see for yourself.

5

FROM THE PLAYING FIELD TO TESTIFYING ON CAPITOL HILL

David Egan is a game changer—well spoken, courteous, a comfortable speaker in front of a large audience. The presentation and David's acceptance speech were magical and the Piper family felt great pride that David was the first recipient [of the Dan Piper Award.] The Pipers and Egans had an opportunity to talk following the ceremony. The philosophical likenesses in experiences raising a child with Down syndrome resonated between the parents of both self-advocates. We all departed Vancouver vowing to keep in touch . . . and keep in touch over the years, we have.

—Sylvia Piper, CEO of Disability Rights Iowa[1]

On the day I testified in front of a U.S. Senate committee, two important things happened. First, I had the full attention of an important and influential group of seasoned senators and was able to testify and discuss the important and serious topic of employment for people with disabilities. Second, I made Senator Al Franken laugh. The former senator from Minnesota, the accomplished comedian and former member of *Saturday Night Live*, laughed at a quip I made on the spot.

I'll never forget that day. It was in 2011, and it just so happened it was that year's Special Olympics Capitol Hill Day. I was one of dozens of Special Olympics athletes from throughout the country who went to the Capitol that day to speak to members of Congress. It's an annual effort to make the impact of Special Olympics clear in the minds of people who provide some of the organization's funding.

More about that in a bit.

A POWERFUL FORCE IN MY LIFE

I have mentioned Special Olympics many times in earlier chapters and the big impact it has had on my life. But the connection between Special Olympics and my speaking at a Senate committee meeting needs a little explaining. You may know that Special Olympics is a worldwide organization with offices in most countries throughout the world. You may know that Special Olympics is all about improving the lives of people with intellectual disabilities. But you may not know that Special Olympics events happen every day of the year and involve much more than sports.

But it starts with sports. Sports develop our mental and physical abilities in ways that help us overcome and challenge our disabilities. That's one reason why Eunice Kennedy Shriver founded Special Olympics in 1968, to give people with intellectual disabilities their own place to train, learn, and compete. But there is more to it than that. The mission of Special Olympics is to show that we *can* train, learn, and compete, to prove to the world that we have gifts that can make a difference. In 1968, a lot of people thought intellectual disabilities made it impossible to learn sport rules, train and grow in our capabilities, strive to win, and feel the hurt of losing. Few people think that now. But few people know how deeply Special Olympics sports improve our lives in far-reaching ways.

Special Olympics sports help us do more in life off the playing field. In coming together for sports, the athletes, families, friends, and volunteers form a welcoming and safe community. It's an environment of warm, encouraging support. It gives us the courage to try harder in everything we do. It's a place that celebrates our abilities, shares our joy, and cheers our accomplishments.

I know that I have a disability, just like many others in this world, but my disability does not get in the way when I train, perform, and compete. It doesn't keep me from working. I take the Metro to work, passing through the card readers, waiting for my train, getting off where I am supposed to, and walking to my office. I earn my paycheck at the office, and then it's back to the Metro to get home. Special Olympics didn't teach me that, but the confidence and determination I gained in Special Olympics sports pays off in many ways. It's a model of inclusion that works on the court, at school, in the workplace, and in any community—anywhere. Everywhere.

LEADERSHIP, HAND IN HAND WITH ADVOCACY

Part of the confidence I learned in Special Olympics is about speaking up for myself. If I can self-advocate, it's not much harder to learn to advocate for others at the same time. That's a form of leadership that Special Olympics values and cultivates in programs throughout the world and in its dozens of chapters in the United States. I mentioned how I accidentally found myself speaking on behalf of Special Olympics at the 1999 World Games. The great thing is that someone at Special Olympics saw that I had done that and invited me to do more. That's the cultivation I mentioned. Between 1999 and 2011, I became a better speaker, leader, and advocate. And that is why I was in that Senate meeting room on Capitol Hill Day 2011.

It was March 2. I had been asked to testify on employment for the Health, Education, Labor, and Pensions Committee, chaired by then-senator Tom Harkin, who I had met earlier with our friend, Sylvia Piper. I was honored and sent my written testimony to Michael Gamel McCormic, his chief of staff, and I was well prepared to give the oral version at the Dirksen Building. It was the first hearing (I always have firsts in my journey) in a series to examine how to improve employment opportunities for people with disabilities.

Employment for the disability community is disappointingly low. Far less than half of people with intellectual disabilities have jobs, and that's a shame in a lot of ways. When someone is employed, they have a sense of purpose and independence, whether they have a disability or not. I have worked since shortly after high school, and I now have a job at SourceAmerica that combines my love of speaking with my passion for advocacy. I can't imagine what my life would be without that challenge, routine, and opportunity to grow and learn. (You'll read more about my work life and how I found my dream job at SourceAmerica later.)

> **Hats Off to the Senator**
>
> I was glad that Senator Harkin was leading the hearing. He was instrumental in passing two landmark pieces of legislation: the Individuals with Disabilities Education Act (IDEA) in 1990 and the Americans with Disabilities Act (ADA) in 1991. These were crucial laws that have improved the lives of people like me. He is a rock star in our community.

The room at the Dirksen Building was packed, with forty people in chairs and more standing at the rear and on the sides. Special Olympics athletes, staff, volunteers, and parents were among the people in the room. Tim Shriver, chairman of Special Olympics International, was there. His brother, Anthony Shriver, chairman of Best Buddies International,[2] was there, too. (Best Buddies improves the daily lives of people with developmental disabilities through friendships and inclusive employment.) There were even more people outside the hearing room who were interested in this testimony. The hearing was televised on C-SPAN. This was big, and it was real. Today was the day one of my dreams would come true, testifying in front of the Senate on Capitol Hill.

Senator Harkin apologized for the small room, asking for more chairs to be brought into the chamber. I could feel the energy of the people in the room and in the hallway. I was excited for this opportunity to finally be where I had dreamed of speaking my entire life—like a statesman on TV. I am sure I had seen this room on C-SPAN and many more like it.

I had always told my mother I would do this one day, and now it was actually happening.

THE EMPLOYMENT CHALLENGE

Senator Harkin laid the foundation with his opening statement: "We are here today to examine the barriers and, most importantly, identify solutions to increase the employment participation rate for all individuals with disabilities."[3] He acknowledged that society's low expectations for individuals with intellectual disabilities means they face the most significant barriers and have the lowest employment among the various disability groups. He also reminded us of his friend Danny Piper, who had Down syndrome like me and worked in a hardware store and for the senator in his office in Iowa. Danny's life was enriched by work, and he changed perceptions of people with intellectual disabilities.

"Employment for persons with disabilities benefits all of society," Senator Harkin said at the beginning of the hearing. "There are great benefits to employing persons with disabilities—for the individual, for the business, and for society at large. So, this hearing is one of the first steps to address this problem of underparticipation in the workforce by persons with disabilities."[4]

Following the opening by Senator Harkin, Senator Johnny Isakson of Georgia spoke up. He said that since the passage of ADA, Americans have been in agreement that it is important to support people with disabilities. It is a bipartisan cause, he said.

I was getting excited about my opportunity to advocate for my fellow athletes on a subject that I had experience in. I was one of four individuals on the panel. I was joined by Joan Evans, director of Wyoming Department of Workforce Services; Randy Lewis, senior vice president of Walgreens, Co., from Deerfield Illinois; and William Kiernan, PhD, director of the Institute for Community Inclusion, from the University of Massachusetts in Boston. I was third to speak. The pressure was on.

Joan Evans spoke first. I liked her quote from President Franklin Roosevelt, who said,

---

A Friend I Never Met

Dan Piper was the first person with Down syndrome to testify in front of Congress, telling his story in support of ADA. The person who made this possible was Senator Tom Harkin, Dan's friend. I was so proud that the senator talked about Danny. Unfortunately, I never met Danny. He died doing what he fought for, for others like him and me—the right to work. Dan died in a pedestrian–automobile accident in 2002 on his way to work. He was thirty-one years old.

I was honored to be the first person to receive the Dan Piper Award from the National Down Syndrome Society (NDSS) in 2006. I met his brother, Larry, and his mom, Sylvia Piper, when they presented me with the award at the World Down Syndrome Convention in Vancouver, Canada. Since then, I have continued that mission in Dan's honor. I have had the privilege to participate in giving the Dan Piper Award with Mrs. Piper in New York City to others who have demonstrated leadership and advocacy in their community.

"No country, however rich, can afford the waste of its human resources. Demoralization caused by vast unemployment is our greatest extravagance. Morally, it is the greatest menace to our social order."

Mr. Lewis went second. (*I'm next!*) He oversees the logistics network and distribution centers, which service seven thousand five hundred stores throughout the country. He spoke about a 2003 Walgreens initiative to build an inclusive workforce.

"Our objectives were straightforward: First, to build a center that was more productive than any we had ever built, with a new foundation of systems, machines, and processes," said Randy.

Second, we wanted to have an inclusive environment where one-third of the workforce was made up of people with disabilities who might not otherwise have a job.

But we also wanted a sustainable business model—an inclusive workplace where people with and without disabilities work side by side, earning the same pay, doing the same jobs, and held to the same productivity and other workplace standards.

That new approach worked, he said. His staff became better managers and leaders, and everyone benefitted. He ended with this comment: "No matter how different we seem, we are more alike than we are different."

His statement resonates with me, as I see my country and the world becoming ever more divided. We must always focus on what brings us together. Disabilities occur in many families, whether rich or poor, liberal or conservative, uneducated or highly educated. They affect people of every race and religion. It's a human condition that can unify us all.

> **Another Friend on Hand**
>
> Just before I spoke, Representative Cathy McMorris Rodgers from the state of Washington came into the chamber. Senator Harkin recognized her and invited her to join the senators at the front of the room.
>
> My brother Marc was an intern for the congresswoman at the time. She is a good friend and a leader for people with disabilities, and cochair of the Congressional Down Syndrome Task Force. Marc had worked behind the scenes to make sure she could join the hearing.

MY TURN

I was next to speak. Senator Harkin welcomed me and said he had read my testimony. He said it was great and called me a role model.

In 2011, I was working as a clerk in the distribution center at Booz Allen Hamilton, a big international consulting firm based in Washington, DC. I had earned my position by showing what I could do in internships and later applying for and securing the job the same way other people do, I said. I stressed the value of inclusion in the workplace. I explained the idea that people with disabilities should be assumed to have diverse abilities and be employable by many companies.

"Employing individuals with intellectual disabilities is a smart business decision and a social responsibility," I said.

I spoke about my job, how I started, and how someone like me can succeed on the job. I talked about the ways in which Special Olympics programs laid the groundwork for me to go from the playing field to employment to advocacy. I quoted Eunice Kennedy Shriver's address at the 1987 World Games in Indiana, where she opened a door for people with intellectual disabilities to do what they dreamed of doing.

"You are the stars, and the world is watching you," she had told the huge crowd in the stadium. She continued:

> By your presence, you send a message to every village, every city, and every nation. You send a message of hope and a message of victory.
>
> The right to play on any playing field, you have earned it. The right to study in any school, you have earned it. The right to hold a job, you have earned it. The right to be anyone's neighbor, you have earned it.

While I was speaking, I could feel the positive vibes in the room. It was buzzing. The support I was getting from the audience in front of me and behind me invigorated me to dig deeper in my delivery of my speech.

The chairman, Senator Harkin, was pleased and said, "You took our breath away. That was a great testimony. Thank you very, very much."

Senator Harkin added that he saw Mr. Lewis of Walgreens paying close attention to what I was saying. "I hope he's not planning a corporate raid on Booz Allen Hamilton," he joked.

The room burst into laughter. I was happy and took a deep breath.

After the witnesses gave their presentations, it was time for questions.

Senator Franken spoke up. He explained he had three other hearings to attend but felt compelled to attend the hearing to hear my testimony.

"In reading it last night, it was spectacular, and then in hearing and seeing you give it, equally spectacular. And so I just had to be here," he commented. He had just visited a community rehabilitation program in Minnesota called AccessAbility. He said he was impressed by the energy of people there. They were happy to be working. He wanted to know if I thought competitive employment was better than sheltered workshops, places set aside for people with disabilities to work.

"Do you think that by being in a competitive, integrated employment that you just get a lot more out of it?" he asked me.

I said yes, because it provides opportunities for growth on the job.

Then he asked me to talk about my mentor, Greg Jones. I shared that he is a role model who offers support and guidance, and doesn't mind joking with me a little.

"Someone joking around with you shows that he respects your sense of humor," Franken said. "And would you say he's funny? When he's joking around with you, is he funny?"

In my years of watching C-SPAN, I had picked up some of the lingo. My mind lit up, and I asked a question that has become a hallmark moment from the event.

"Is this for the record?"

Senator Franken and the entire room exploded with laughter.

Playing along, the comedian and Minnesota senator said, "We'll strike it. You don't have to answer on that one."

My moment had arrived, and I loved every minute of it.

Senator Mike Enzi, cochair of the HELP committee, thanked everyone on the panel and complimented me for "stealing the show." Senator Harkin summed it up by stressing that we need to change the way we think about employing people with disabilities. He said students with disabilities should be prepared in school and have the expectation to find work in their communities.

"Everyone can achieve a little bit more. Everybody can do something a little bit better," he said.

> And I think we have failed in our education system and in our career opportunities to really provide that kind of stimulation to young people with disabilities.
>
> Mr. Egan, it's been a delight having you here. Thank you very much for what you've added to this hearing and what you've added to our knowledge base.

The testimony and the hearing were a big success. Everyone was energized and determined to make employment a priority for adults with intellectual disabilities. I walked out of the chamber more determined than ever to make employment a key theme in my advocacy and find ways of making it a reality for many others.

A VALUABLE PART OF THE COMMUNITY

Working for pay is a big part of ordinary adult life. It's more than earning a paycheck, however. Our work lets us show what we can do. It lets us build skills and grow our confidence, knowledge, and wisdom. When we work in the community, we are a valuable part of the community. That feeling of being included and welcomed is missing for many people with disabilities. Being at home means being out of the flow of community life. Being at work, having friends, knowing what part you play are key to feeling fully included. I learned to be truly independent at work, away from the supporting hands of my family.

The thing some people don't get is that a disability hampers you in one area, not all areas. My intellectual disability means I learn at a slower pace than most people, but I can do plenty of other things just as well as anyone else. The accommodations I need most are simply patience and time.

When Mrs. Shriver said, "The right to hold a job, you have earned it," she was talking about the right to hold any job that suits us. There are jobs that don't suit me, and that's true for everyone. That's why big companies have CEOs, accountants, salespeople, engineers, janitors, project managers, artists, and entire offices full of people who are good at their job but not every job.

My job fits *me*. I'm doing it because my company was open to hiring me to do work that I can do and do well. If more companies did that, unexpected benefits would certainly happen.

So, I'm inviting you to think about where you work. Don't think about a role for a person with a disability. Think about roles for people with particular abilities and open your eyes to the possibilities.

6

EMPLOYMENT

"One of Them and Not Just One among Them"

> Work provides more than a paycheck. It brings dignity and community. When businesses open job opportunities to men and women with disabilities, everyone benefits—the individual, the company, and society at large.
>
> —Dr. Ralph Shrader, former CEO of Booz Allen Hamilton[1]

My family taught me that work is part of life. Early on, even at the age of two, I learned to put away my toys, and I even tried to empty the dishwasher. I climbed onto the open door of the dishwasher and reached in to grab the clean glasses. Nothing broke!

As a child, it seemed normal to contribute as everyone else was, and I was proud of my work. I know now that employment is a complex issue for people with Down syndrome and other intellectual disabilities. Like many things in my life, the work landscape has changed a lot and for the better. When I was born in the 1970s, the best many people with Down syndrome could hope for was doing repetitive tasks in a carefully controlled place set aside for such work. It must have seemed absurd at the time to think that someone could be like me, independently

Government Benefits and Making It Work

Part of what makes the employment situation tricky is the fact that many people with intellectual and developmental disabilities need to rely on government benefits. I will highlight that I never used government benefits because I had a competitive job starting in high school and am on my parents' health insurance for life. That is a complex topic that is too much to get into here, so my experience does not include having to make that balance work.

71

working side by side with people in a big office, making decisions about my day-to-day work and getting paid a regular wage. Things are better now, and I am one example. But there are many bright, capable people with Down syndrome sitting at home or doing jobs that don't challenge them. Why is that? I think part of it has to do with confidence. Maybe the people with more self-confidence will try for jobs that others might not. And businesses are looking for people who have confidence in what they can do.

I can tell you (with confidence) that self-confidence is not something I struggle with. I am outgoing, curious, and love to talk to people. I like to try new things, and I am never shy about giving my opinion.

The other part is that companies need to be open to hiring people with disabilities. All the confidence in the world won't get you a job if companies won't consider your application. In the previous chapter, U.S. senators cited statistics about the low rate of employment of people with disabilities. For people like me, people with intellectual disabilities, the employment rate is very low. I am hopeful that my story will help change the hiring practices of employers.

My work life has been unusual in some ways, but it's fairly common now to see people with Down syndrome doing all kinds of work. I mentioned earlier that since I was born, the standard practice of sending babies with Down syndrome to institutions for lifelong care has pretty much ended. The amazing changes that resulted from children having loving environments full of enriching experiences include a blossoming of skills, potential, and achievement. Society expects more of us, but there is even more we can do than most people believe. Work is the next frontier for us to show what we can do.

Many Pluses for Employers

I want to do what I can to help others with intellectual disabilities launch their own careers. I talk about this often when I do my public speaking. But no one can get a job simply by wishing or asking for it. Opportunities need to be there, and they won't be there unless employers see the value of hiring us. There are many benefits that are not obvious. I believe that people who work with someone with a disability become better at their job by learning to explain things in simpler terms. Being with people who think differently leads to learning new ways of motivation. Everyone brings new insights to the workplace, and we are no different. Work is about productivity and making money, but it is also about human interactions and learning to work as a team. I think people with disabilities help uncover human values and, by doing so, improve the work environment and company culture.

I am proud to say that because of an inclusive life and education, as well as career-transition internships, my disability has not prevented me from working in competitive jobs. I was given many opportunities to overcome the challenges I faced with Down syndrome. And now, nothing matters more to me than demonstrating to others that people like me are employable. I am proud to claim my twenty-plus years of experience in competitive, integrated employment. I know there are many things I can do well because I have had the chance to try many things. Some I was not so good at, but others I did very well. Every chance to try something new is a chance to gain more confidence in myself.

Simply being employed meant the world to me at first. It has made my life fulfilling in many ways, just as it does for everyone else. And as my career progressed, I knew I could learn more and contribute more. That would make anyone feel good about themselves and make them feel valuable.

I have loved the feeling of being part of companies where everyone plays a part in business success. It's like being on a sports team in some ways. There are challenges when you have a real job, so it's not all fun and smiles. Having a work life like other people's means facing frustrations, along with the benefits of work. If you want to work and be challenged along the way, you need to be able to accept that some days will be hard. You will make mistakes, and you will be told about them and asked to do better. But bottom line, it's great to feel included because of what I can do and not feel I am there simply as an act of corporate social responsibility.

Like many people, my work life started with chores at home.

CHORES, CHORES, AND MORE CHORES

I liked to imitate what people are doing when I was little. My parents have photos of me trying to vacuum the apartment where we lived. As little as I was, I managed to push it around and make the big noise just like my dad did. I thought that was the point, and it looked like great fun. It became less fun when I learned that the point was to make the apartment cleaner and that you had to run it everywhere. But back then, it was a thrill to hear the noise and feel like I was helping. I liked that feeling of confidence and contributing to the household's day-to-day work.

Real chores came soon enough. Expectations of responsibility were not excused by having a disability. I was the oldest of four children. Each fall, when it was time to rake leaves in our backyard, all four of us helped Dad clean up for winter.

Early on, I started helping set the dinner table every night. (That is still my job more than three decades later. I'm *very* good at it.) I helped with laundry and keeping the house clean, just like everyone else in my family. It was important to contribute and work as a team.

I have vivid memories of Teresa, Miranda, Marc, and me helping Dad take down a big maple tree in front of the house. I remember us standing on the roof with ropes in our hands as my Dad provided instructions on how we were going to uproot the massive, old tree towering over our house. It was challenging and a little frightening, but the big crash as the tree smashed into the ground was a scary, big thrill. We had done it!

The four of us then planted new cherry and magnolia trees, which I continue to admire each morning looking out our kitchen bay window. We also planted a pine tree, my Mom's favorite, in the back of the house. We decorate it every year for Christmas. Throughout the years, we've had to buy longer and longer strings of colored lights as the tree has gotten taller and fuller. The decorated tree looks stunning when snow covers the branches full of glowing Christmas lights.

Speaking of snow, every time it snowed, everyone in the household helped shovel it away. After Dad, I was the strongest in the family, so he really relied on

---

The Empty Peanut

I have fond memories of my younger brother Marc raking side by side with me. He was known as the "empty peanut" around the house because he was twelve years younger than me and couldn't contribute the way I could at the time. I felt like a useful big brother to him. He's now all grown up and married, so he takes the lead with any work in the yard or helping Dad with fixing things around the house. He visits us regularly to check if we need any help. He is now a full peanut.

Public Transportation Skills

Both of my parents worked full time, so I had to learn to take a public bus to internships and later to work. Mom went on the bus with me a few times to show me where to get on and off. She taught me about crossing roads. After a week of practice, I was ready to do it on my own: paying for the ride and getting on and off at the right bus stops. For a while my mom would drive behind the bus to make sure I was okay since there were no cell phones back then. Also, my mentor, Greg Jones, would wait for me on the sidewalk in the early days to make sure I was safe. I have taken the bus and the Metro train now for more than twenty years, and I am at ease with it.

my help. He needed my support for various tasks throughout the different seasons, which made me feel useful and good. I learned so many different skills. Every new thing I mastered made the next thing easier to try and take on. I loved getting the backyard ready for fun picnics and parties. One year, for Father's Day, my siblings, Mom, and I gave him a photo album of his "workforce house crew," the four kids who helped indoors and outdoors. We had different jobs, but we were one united crew working as a team. No matter how complex or simple the job, I learned how to do it and gave it my best.

To be honest, however, there were many times I did not feel like helping. I think that is normal, especially as a child whose mindset is often solely focused on having fun. Chores were not *always* fun. But I learned that chores are always necessary to make the house run as it should. Through chores done around the house, I learned that everyone needs to pull their own weight and contribute to the family. Only after that you can sit back, relax, and enjoy. Chores are duties, and doing your duty is something you need to learn early in life. For me at least, that life skill has lasted a lifetime.

LEARNING ABOUT WORK AT SCHOOL

My experience with work outside the house began in high school and continued in programs after high school once I graduated with a special diploma. I learned such important office skills as filing, sorting, copying, faxing, mailing, and delivering documents to people. I got experience in cooking tasks—take-out restaurant, cleaning, waiting, busing, stacking. I took classes on outdoor maintenance skills that reminded me of my chores at home. Thanks to the confidence my mom and dad fostered in me as a child, I had no fears about trying new things. At some point, I realized that what my mom and dad called *chores*, businesses call *work*.

Unpaid internships were part of the public school's program. I got good on-the-job experience at my internships, and those set me up for success when I got a real paying job. Fortunately, I had a long-term internship at Booz Allen Hamilton. One of the company's managers, Barbara Haight, helped coordinate the internship, which put young people to work in the company's mail room in the distribution center.

"The minute David arrived, his trademark smile broke the ice with his new colleagues, and I knew we were on the road to success for years to come," Barbara recalled in an e-mail to me.[2]

Barbara got an award as manager of the year early in the internship program, which was a partnership between Booz Allen Hamilton, the Marriott Foundation for People with Disabilities, and the Fairfax County school system. President George H. W. Bush presented the award to Barbara. She remembers being thrilled to meet President Bush because he had signed the Americans with Disabilities Act.

"I remember standing on the stage in a ballroom filled with hundreds of attendees, but what I really focused on was seeing David's face sporting that ear-to-ear grin," Barbara wrote. "The partnership was successful enough that once David graduated, he was hired by Booz Allen directly."[3]

> **Getting to Know One Another**
>
> The folks at Booz Allen Hamilton had little-to-no experience working with people with disabilities or special needs when I did my internship there. Felicia Bussey, my immediate supervisor, took it upon herself to teach me everything there was to know about being a clerk, and she was wonderful. She believed in me and wanted me to succeed. During the internship, Fairfax County provided a job coach to support my training, but Felicia preferred to show me the ropes herself. The coach stopped in regularly and could see how much progress I was making working with Felicia. Her hands-on approach worked so well that the job coach had little to do but say, "Well done!"

MY FIRST REAL JOB WAS A TURNING POINT

I was hired after being invited to apply for a full-time job opening in the distribution center. That was a big deal! It was not common for someone with an intellectual disability to get an opportunity like that in 1998. That experience was a turning point in my life. It was the start of a journey of competitive employment and the launching of a successful career.

The mail room is part of the distribution center, so everything I learned in my internship at Booz Allen Hamilton came in handy from the very first day of my new job. I had learned to be on time and fill out a timesheet. I had learned to establish a schedule for the day and stick to it. I had done my job well enough to impress the staff. We were both starting something new. In a way, it was an experiment that both Booz Allen Hamilton and I wanted to be a big success. And it was.

For me, it started as a gesture by the company to do the right thing for people in the community with disabilities. Companies who care about what happens beyond their walls feel a sense of responsibility. And that is part of the reason I had the chance to do the internship in the first place. But when I showed what I could do, it became clear that I was contributing in a way that any business would value. It changed from a gesture of goodwill to an example of good business sense. I was a full-time employee, with not only pay and benefits, but also the responsibility to perform well and accept constructive advice at review time.

I found out that being a competitive employee brought challenges of many kinds, along with the rewards of pay and satisfaction of a job well done. With high expectations come the challenge of meeting them. And when I met them, I had the confidence to aim a little higher.

HIGH EXPECTATIONS ARE A SIGN OF RESPECT

As the years passed, I continued to learn new skills. I learned to use new computer systems and follow the instructions of a manifest, to make sure outgoing packages had everything Booz Allen Hamilton clients needed. I also learned to switch from mail room duties to helping out in the supply room when I had downtime. I learned a lot of new skills, and it really started to sink in that many situations required different solutions. I have to admit that learning so much so quickly, and with a different supervisor, was hard for me. It pushed me to my limits. While I gained new skills, I missed my supervisor Felicia Bussey and her hands-on engagement with me. I had a rough time adjusting to the new supervisor, but with the help of my mentor, Greg Jones, and the distribution center senior manager, I was able to adapt and thrive.

The senior manager in the mail room was Isaac Webb. He was kind to me from the very first day I arrived. Throughout the years of my employment at the company, I grew close to Mr. Webb. He had a good heart and cared about his staff, especially me. I enjoyed it when he would call me into his office for a chat. He took the time to get to know me and helped me grow professionally. He knew I loved to talk, so he gently directed me to be alert to signs that a conversation should be ending. He was honest that way and gave me constructive tips to improve my job performance. He recognized me when I did well and often high-fived me. He knew the senior executives were proud of having an individual with an intellectual disability working in the mail room and being treated like other employees.

I learned it all, and then I felt I was thriving again with new skills, new understanding, and a new level of respect from my managers and coworkers. I also gained a new point of view about what you might call the "real world of work." Adults ask people in high school what their plans are for the "real world." I kind of wondered what that meant, because to me, school *was* the real world, too. But now I understand that school was a place of nurturing, individual attention, and patient teaching. In the world of business, you need to use what you've learned in school to work more independently than before. It's not sink or swim, but you are expected to do your job with less and less support as time goes on.

How well you do depends on not only your own confidence, but also the attitudes of the people where you work. If people don't expect much, they won't ask much, and the job will stay the same with no new challenges. Without challenges, no one can grow in skill, understanding, and respect, as I did at Booz Allen Hamilton. Some employers may worry that telling employees they are doing something wrong is unkind. They might not realize that constructive criticism is a sign of respect. I am glad that my managers gave me the respect of telling me when I did something wrong or needed to do something differently. Everyone needs to feel frustration and use those feelings to

Even More to Be Proud Of

In addition to supporting me as a staff employee, Booz Allen Hamilton supported an organization I love, Special Olympics. Senior partners of the company were on the board of directors of Special Olympics Virginia. The company was a big sponsor of the Special Olympics Virginia Winter Games. The company also supported the international arm of Special Olympics. Booz Allen Hamilton helped underwrite the costs for a global meeting of Special Olympics athlete leaders in the Netherlands. The partnership was strong, and I was proud of my company.

drive accomplishment. If a company respects you, its employees will take time to invest in you. They will ask more of you than what you are doing. They will question your approach to tasks in helpful ways. If you're an employee, these conversations can feel uncomfortable. You might not like it when you are in the middle of it. But that's what the real world is all about, and that's the only way you will learn what your limits are. And once you know your limits, you can go about exceeding them.

None of that can happen without good people around you, and at Booz Allen Hamilton, I had good people all around me. I was a success story for the company. It was a source of pride that someone with an intellectual disability could hold a job, grow in the job, and be welcomed and accepted by everyone. My training paid off in many little ways. Since I knew my way around the distribution center and supply room, I took the initiative to combine what I knew. I asked people to let me know what supplies they needed, and I brought the supplies with their mail. I knew they were busy, and I wanted to save them time.

As a result of the support from every level of the company, I felt like a full team member. I felt I truly belonged because the company cared about my personal and professional development. I received full benefits, time off, and an annual 360-degree assessment like everyone else. I went to required training and participated in all-hands meetings, where the employees and stakeholders of the organization would hear from the senior managers and be updated on important events and milestones. I was also invited to yearly corporate events and holiday parties. The point I want to make is that they included me in all the activities. I was sponsored for conferences for my professional development. I was an equal in all matters and well acquainted with the staff and clients. I was *one of them and not just one among them*. I felt respected, I felt that people listened to me, and I felt my opinions mattered. That inspired me to contribute as much as I could. That is such a great feeling.

A MYSTERIOUS REQUEST

Getting a job is sometimes easier than sustaining a successful career. The culture of the company is important to being truly included. It's also important to have a supervisor who knows you and speaks up for you when things become complicated. I faced a situation that could have been a bad one, and my supervisor took careful steps to protect me. I'll tell you what happened.

During the holidays, the distribution center is busier than usual with packages and deliveries. Booz Allen Hamilton hired temporary employees and contractors to help with the extra work. Some of them understood and accepted that I was a permanent staff employee who did my job well. But other people couldn't see past the obvious fact that I had Down syndrome. They resented the fact that I was a staff employee when they were not. And they thought they could blame me for things when they made mistakes.

One day, my supervisor, Felicia, called my mother and said, "Tell David not to come to work tomorrow."

My mother was worried and asked why, but Felicia replied, "Just trust me."

So I stayed home that day. We wondered all day what this mysterious request was all about.

What Mom and I did not know is that I had been accused of misplacing or stealing packages containing cell phones, tablets, and laptops. Felicia was confident that I was not involved. She made sure I was at home, and when packages went missing on that day, she could prove it wasn't me who was responsible. My name was cleared.

It's important to have a supervisor and a culture that treats people with developmental disabilities with respect and trust. Felicia took the time to solve the problem in a way that was fair to everyone, including me. She was not the only one who supported me. Isaac Webb, Derek Moyer, Felicia Bussey, and Greg Jones were among my closest supporters.

My Mentor and Friend

Greg Jones, a senior employee in the distribution center, became my friend and mentor. Greg was a role model for me, and he still is. Everyone in the workplace needs a mentor like Greg.

In a video interview on employment sponsored by the National Down Syndrome Society (NDSS), "Launch: Careers for People with Down Syndrome," Greg said, "He worked real hard to help me to understand his needs, and I worked real hard to get the staff to understand the needs that we have to provide to him. . . . He is a positive part of society, adding value."[4]

I enjoyed interacting and socializing with Greg. He was the guy I could joke with, and he understood my needs and sense of humor. I trusted his guidance at all times. It meant a lot to me when, in May 2003, he traveled to New York City (Greg does not like to travel but made an exception for me) to see me receive the NDSS's Voices award, presented to me by Senator Hillary Clinton.

Dr. Ralph Shrader, who was CEO and chairman of Booz Allen Hamilton, called us "heroes" when he received an advocacy award. "They rise to the test: Charmed lives and smooth seas don't make heroes. . . . Greg coached David and encouraged his community activities. . . . Greg was most instrumental in allowing David to achieve his success."[5]

CHANGES AND OPPORTUNITIES

In 2013, Booz Allen Hamilton outsourced facilities and logistics operations to CBRE, an international real estate company, which included the distribution center in the same facility. The Booz Allen Hamilton distribution center employees had to reapply for the job if they did not want to leave.

Greg Jones, my mentor, helped me apply for the clerk job at CBRE. I got the job after submitting my resume and having face-to-face interviews.

My duties didn't change much. I was still working in the distribution center, but I was doing it as an employee of CBRE. I worked for CBRE for about three years before an exciting and historic opportunity came my way. I applied for a position as a Joseph P. Kennedy Jr. Public Policy Fellow and was chosen in 2015. I was going to work on Capitol Hill with a congressional subcommittee and work with NDSS on its advocacy efforts in Washington, DC. I was the first person with an intellectual disability to have this honor. (I will tell you much more about this in a later chapter.)

CBRE was supportive and proud of my fellowship. They gave me a year's leave without pay and the reassurance of keeping my job upon my return. When the fellowship was over, CBRE took me back for a few months, but unfortunately the distribution center contract ended in the fall of 2016.

All of us received a notice that we needed to find new jobs, and we had just two weeks to do so. It was a shock for all of us, me included. Everyone knows the first thing to do when you lose a job is to start networking. I had made many contacts on Capitol Hill and through Special Olympics, but it was a person I had never met who made the crucial connection for me—and with timing that seemed heaven-sent. Joe O'Brien was an usher at our church and an executive at CBRE. He had read an article about my fellowship. One Sunday morning, after many casual hellos and smiles throughout the years, he recognized me and introduced himself. When he heard my job was ending, he offered to connect me with other people he knew at CBRE.

Widening Choices for Jobs

People I know in the Down syndrome community are finding that there are more and more ways to have jobs and careers. Parents are taking the lead to create opportunities when the conventional job market doesn't. People with Down syndrome may work at a family restaurant, coffee shop, or catering service. Some families have created new businesses and given their children with Down syndrome real jobs where they promote and sell their own line of clothing or artworks. Families can see potential and talent that many employers simply don't take time to explore. With family-run small businesses, their loved ones can pursue their dreams in a rewarding and inclusive workplace. Also, some individuals are taking the path of celebrities in modeling, acting, and public speaking. Wherever we work, we add value.

"None of us should be defined by our limitations," Joe said in an e-mail he sent after hearing I was writing a book.

> David is truly defined by his abilities and accomplishments. When I heard that David was at a transition point in his career, I knew I had to help. It wasn't so much that CBRE had enough room under its tent to find David another position; rather, I knew CBRE could *not afford* to lose someone with David's talents, drive, and enthusiasm.[6]

With Joe's help, my networking paid off. I got an interview and earned a new position as a CBRE facility coordinator at the Booz Allen Hamilton building in McLean, Virginia. It was a familiar kind of job, stocking kitchens with coffee supplies, filling printers with paper, and posting flyers throughout the facility. I was grateful to have the job, but after being on Capitol Hill as a Kennedy fellow, I wanted something more.

The CBRE management team was kind to me and thrilled to learn about my involvement with Special Olympics. CBRE gave me leave to participate in the Special Olympics 2017 World Winter Games in Austria. And that is where my love of meeting people and networking really paid off. I met a lot of people in Austria, and two of them, John Kelly and Shane Kanady, were senior managers of a big U.S. nonprofit called SourceAmerica. They were there as part of their development of a partnership with Special Olympics. While in Austria, John and Shane took part in panel discussions about employment of people with intellectual disabilities. I spoke up with a question during their panel discussion, and they introduced themselves to me afterward.

One thing led to another, as they say, and SourceAmerica offered me a position as a community relations specialist in its gov-

---

About SourceAmerica

SourceAmerica's mission is to "provide employment choices for individuals with disabilities through the nonprofit agency community. Many of these nonprofit agency members rely on contracting through SourceAmerica and the AbilityOne Program." SourceAmerica's goal is to help ensure that "all people with a disability have a choice of careers, are celebrated for their abilities, and are recognized for creating a more vibrant work environment." The organization puts it this way: "We're proud to play a role in helping people with disabilities find meaningful jobs. Because we believe that anyone who's willing to work should have the opportunity to do so—that's what the American Dream is all about."[7] There's a lot more information about this great company at its website, https://www.sourceamerica.org/.

ernment affairs department. I started in September 2017. In 2019, I took on a different role as a partnerships coordinator on SourceAmerica's Workforce Development Team. It is such a perfect place to work after my year with the public policy fellowship and the years I had spent as an athlete spokesman for Special Olympics. I can put my advocacy skills to work on a daily basis. SourceAmerica's mission is very much like my goal in advocacy: to break down barriers so people with disabilities can find meaningful work they enjoy. These latest employment positions with the fellowship and at SourceAmerica have been challenging, but they have taught me a lot about work and contributing as an individual to team projects.

UNIFIED IN SPORT, WORK, AND LIFE

In so many ways, my life's experience prepared me for the work at SourceAmerica. The project Shane and I worked on was a partnership between Special Olympics and SourceAmerica called WorkUnified. Shane and John were in Austria during the World Winter Games, as part of their work on that initiative. John was director of government affairs then; Shane was director of special projects for the Government Affairs department.

WorkUnified combines the employment focus of SourceAmerica and the PlayUnified Sports initiative at Special Olympics. The idea of Unified Sports is to have people who don't have disabilities playing on teams with people with intellectual disabilities. Coming together as a team and competing against other unified teams has a way of bringing out the best in everyone. The overall goal of WorkUnified is to increase inclusion of people with disabilities in their communities. Between the two organizations, we covered the world of work and the world of sports. What a great match!

I had years of firsthand experience as a Special Olympics athlete, including playing Unified Sports. Combining that with my experience in the workforce made me the perfect person to work on the WorkUnified partnership. Shane and I showcased the initiative in 2018, during the Special Olympics USA Games in Seattle, and at the Special Olympics fiftieth anniversary celebration in Chicago that same year. We gave our project a catchy name, "Journey of Employment."[8]

The WorkUnified partnership debuted at the USA Games. We wanted a lot of people to know about it, so we walked from place to place at the Games with big posters on our backs. We wanted athletes, coaches, families, and others to know that we were there with an inclusive message about employment. The promotion led to an all-day Journey of Employment meeting. It was the first time there had been a job fair as part of a Special Olympics USA Games. I was the emcee, along with John Kelly. We were both excited about what was going to happen that day.

The first stop on the journey was a short coaching session with employment experts from SourceAmerica and its network of nonprofits. Candidates—Special Olympics athletes from throughout the United States—learned how to share their talents with potential employers. They got interview tips and career advice. Many employers were there, for example, Microsoft, Bank of America, Kaiser Permanente, Amazon, Boeing, Brooks Running Company, Starbucks, the city of Seattle, King County, Walmart, and more. Athletes at the job fair heard from employees and employers. They heard perspectives on recruiting people with intellectual disabilities and making the workplace more inclusive.

I also shared my own story, highlighting how my experience with Special Olympics sports prepared me in some ways for the opportunities that came later. Shane agreed.

"Having [David] as a spokesperson for both sides of the partnership is exciting and important, as it helps to advance our shared goals. David is a tremendous advocate for the missions of both organizations," he said.[9]

I can't help feeling proud about what I have done in my life. I took on chores as a toddler before I even really knew what the point of dishwashing and vacuuming were. The idea of work as a part of life grew on me in high school. And when I knew I wanted to be an advocate for the employment of people with Down syndrome, I focused my goals on just that. I needed help along the way. I was lucky. People saw that I was capable of learning and growing. That's one of the things holding back many people with intellectual disabilities: the belief that we can't learn new things and then learn more.

Part of what has made my work success possible is having confidence in myself. I learned it from parents who let me take on challenges throughout my life. I learned it from Special Olympics, where sports training, discipline, and competition offer unending opportunities to learn and grow. Every job I had showed me and others that I could contribute in my own valuable way. I would never have been working on Capitol Hill had I not gained the confidence to apply for the fellowship. And I might not have found my job at SourceAmerica if I had been too shy to ask a question in a big public meeting.

My work life—and this chapter—begin and end with the idea of confidence. You can't build confidence without taking on challenges. And you can't take on challenges unless someone believes in you enough to let you try. Trying means risking failure. But people say failure is the best teacher. Maybe you can't learn unless you fail a few times.

Throughout my life, people gave me the dignity of learning through taking on challenges that had a risk of failure. I hope that parents, teachers, and employers will think about ways they can offer that dignity to the people with disabilities in their lives.

7

DARING TO DREAM

David Egan is a pioneer. Like all pioneers, David's will and tenacity to venture—and lead others—into new directions requires vision, courage, hard work, sacrifice, and passion. David's character is richly supplied with all of those traits. Also like other pioneers, David has learned that the path is often not an easy, nor clearly evident, one. In my experience, David sees those challenges not as roadblocks, but rather as newly discovered ways to lead. . . . It is David's "so what if nobody else has done this yet, why can't I?" attitude, coupled with a determined spirit, that drives him to such successes and milestones. This paradigm-busting approach seems to be a guiding principle and practice for David . . . and with great results.

—David Thomason, mentor[1]

"Do you want me to change the channel for you?" my mom asked. It seemed to be a natural question for a sixth grader who was watching C-SPAN congressional briefings on TV.

"No, I want to watch this," I said. "I want to go to Capitol Hill one day and give speeches."

My mother was quite surprised. My favorite things to watch on TV were usually sports shows. But I had another side, too. Seeing people in Congress making speeches to declare their views and persuade others made a deep impression on me. I loved the spotlight, even as a little kid, and those members of Congress definitely had the spotlight when they spoke. But I also loved the idea of speaking up for what you believe in. I don't remember exactly, but maybe some part of me wanted to speak up for myself. I knew by then that I had Down syndrome. I knew also that some people didn't see me as capable and valuable. I loved speaking up in school—sometimes in a disruptive way. Back then, I didn't know that I had the makings of an advocate stirring inside me.

I see now that the idea of giving a speech on Capitol Hill was the first way I saw myself as an advocate. It was a dream forming in my imagination. I didn't know what it would take to make that dream come true. All I knew was that I wanted to do it, and C-SPAN was full of examples of the power of persuasion.

C-SPAN showed me that speaking up is a good thing. It can change people's minds and helps get things done. We had studied U.S. government in school, and C-SPAN was like a private window into the world of politics. So, let's not go changing that channel, Mom!

WHAT CAN I DO FOR MY COUNTRY?

When I turned eighteen, my dad asked me what I wanted to do in life. I didn't hesitate. I told him I wanted to help the causes of people with disabilities. By then, I had thought about it enough to know my dream was to do something meaningful for those of us with intellectual disabilities. As President John F. Kennedy said, "Ask not what your country can do for you, ask what you can do for your country."

But what? I didn't have more than a desire to do something when Dad asked the question. Now, I know what I can do, and I am doing it. It has been a process to get to where I am, but big things changed for me in the last several years. Some were things I strived for. Others came by lucky chance. It's still amazing and thrilling to me that I was chosen as a Joseph P. Kennedy Jr. Public Policy Fellow and a Special Olympics Sargent Shriver International Global Messenger in the same year. One took me to the halls and chambers of Capitol Hill. The other took me to countries throughout the world. I will tell you about both.

But first, let me tell you about my hero, Eunice Kennedy Shriver. What she did for her country, and the world, is astounding.

She was the sister of President Kennedy, late senator and U.S. attorney general Robert F. Kennedy, and late senator Ted Kennedy of Massachusetts. She was the founder of Special Olympics, a mission of hers driven by the experience of her sister Rosemary. Mrs. Shriver wanted to overturn the way society understood the abilities and humanity of people with intellectual disabilities. Rosemary had an intellectual disability, and despite her family's wealth and status, Rosemary was shunned and turned away by most

Me at three months old with my mom and dad. I was their first child. They were graduate students at the University of Wisconsin and new to being parents. But they had already resolved to do their best for me. *Courtesy of the Egan Family*

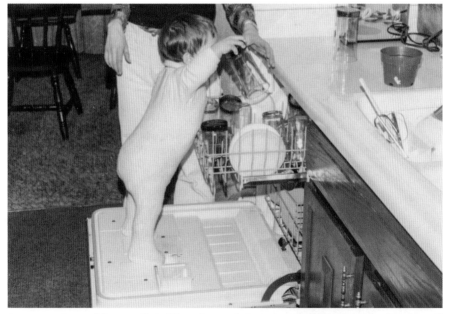

As soon as I was able to walk, I did my best to help out around the house. In this case, all I did was make my mom nervous about the glasses. But to me, I was just doing what I saw other people do. *Courtesy of the Egan Family*

I was fully included in—and a founding member of—the Waisman Early Childhood Program. Mainstreaming for kids like me with Down syndrome was a new idea in 1979. It was a great start for me to build my independence and social skills with other kids. *Courtesy of the Egan Family*

Me posing with my sister Teresa in Stoughton, Wisconsin, at a Fourth of July party at the home of the Rosenbaum family, who hosted a group of international students. I was three and a half, and she was one and a half. Although I was older, Teresa was a smart girl and learned things quickly. *Courtesy of the Egan Family*

In our backyard in Vienna, Virginia. As the big brother, I was often in charge of minding my brother Marc and my sister Miranda. We loved playing basketball, and we still play together sometimes. Both siblings are involved with Special Olympics. *Courtesy of the Egan Family*

Parker Ramsdell and Ginny Theisen were my swim coaches when I started swimming for Special Olympics. Parker was just a teenager when he volunteered to coach me. With his help, my times got faster and faster. My medals were pretty much all the same color: gold. *Courtesy of the Egan Family*

Tim Shriver, chairman of the Special Olympics, congratulates me on my Joseph P. Kennedy Jr. Public Policy Fellowship. Special Olympics has made me a better athlete and a stronger leader. At right is Representative Cathy McMorris Rodgers of Washington state, cochair of the Down Syndrome Task Force in Congress—and a big supporter of mine. *Courtesy of Will Schermerhorn*

My trophy and medals case was made by Brother Eugene Bilodeau, a Canadian Franciscan friar who befriended my mom while she was growing up in Jerusalem. Papa Gene was an accomplished carpenter and a woodcarving master. *Courtesy of Will Schermerhorn*

I had the full attention of the room during my testimony for the U.S. Senate Health, Education, Labor, and Pensions Committee in 2011. I told the senators that employment is a social responsibility and a good business decision. *Courtesy of Special Olympics*

Me talking to then-senator Tom Harkin of Iowa after I testified about employment for people with disabilities. Senator Harkin was a champion of promoting the civil rights of people with disabilities during his ten years in the U.S. Senate. *Courtesy of the Egan Family*

My sister Miranda posing with me and her son, Mason. In addition to being his uncle, I'm also his godfather. *Courtesy of Will Schermerhorn*

David Thomason, right, has been my mentor and good friend for many years. This photo shows us on Capitol Hill, planning to meet with members of U.S. Congress, chatting with a congressional staff member. *Courtesy of the Egan Family*

Felicia Bussey was my first supervisor at Booz Allen Hamilton's distribution center. She guided me with a kind, hands-on approach. She also stood up for me when I really needed it. *Courtesy of the Egan Family*

I played a key role in the Journey of Employment, a partnership between SourceAmerica and Special Olympics, at the 2018 Special Olympics USA Games in Seattle, Washington. *Courtesy of Special Olympics*

In my job with SourceAmerica, I work with people in a variety of departments. I love working with technology and people who understand how important it is for people with disabilities to have meaningful work. At SourceAmerica, I have both, plus the opportunity to do public speaking. *Courtesy of Will Schermerhorn*

My big, wonderful family gathered in Greece for the marriage of my brother, Marc, and Juline Kaleyias. From left: my brother-in-law Matthew Philipp; my sister Teresa; me; my mom Kathleen; my brother Marc; my sister-in-law Juline; my dad John; my sister Miranda; and my brother-in-law Travis. *Courtesy of the Egan Family*

of the professionals they turned to for help. Mrs. Shriver founded Special Olympics in 1968, to prove to the world that people with intellectual disabilities were capable and competitive athletes. And if we could show our gifts through sports, we might open the eyes of people to see that we could do much more.

As I see it, Mrs. Shriver was fighting for me, too, even though I was born years after the founding of Special Olympics. She fought for our human and civil rights, and brought it to the attention of her brother—the president—and Congress. When she had a goal, she didn't let anything stand in her way.

I was with my family at a ceremony honoring her contributions to the children of the United States in 2008. The National Institute of Child Health and Human Development was being renamed to add "Eunice Kennedy Shriver" to its official name.

Her brother, Senator Ted Kennedy, spoke. He said it was difficult to say no to her.

"I guess you could say that Eunice has a talent for getting her way," he said. "And lucky for all of us, 'her way' is to make the world a better place for people with disabilities—and she's been doing that with incredible success for more than sixty years."[2]

Those words resonate with me. Mrs. Shriver was the greatest advocate for our cause, and I wanted to follow in her footsteps. She died in 2009, but she still inspires me to do great things and never give up. I talked about how she changed the world when the *New York Times* interviewed me and called me "one of her friends." A photo of me and Mrs. Shriver accompanied the article.[3]

Did I dare dream of doing what others thought was impossible? Mrs. Shriver's life was dotted with achieving things people thought were impossible. My life was better because she dared to do what she dreamed. So I would, too. And that is why I pursued becoming a Joseph. P. Kennedy Jr. Public Policy Fellow.

CAN I DO THIS?

Mrs. Shriver knew that one way to improve the lives of people like me is by influencing the process of making laws. The Joseph P. Kennedy Jr. Public Policy Fellowship aimed to cultivate strong leaders who could do just that on behalf of people with intellectual disabilities.

I had met several former Kennedy fellowship honorees: Michael McMorris, director of the National Disability Institute; Michael Gamel-McCormick, PhD, associate director of the Center for Disabilities Studies and a professor in the Department of Human Development and Family Studies at the University of Delaware[4]; and Dr. Karen Summar, a pediatrician and medical professional who was a legislative staff member for Representative Cathy McMorris Rodgers of Washington.[5] They piqued my curiosity and encouraged me to apply, even though no one with an intellectual disability had been named a fellow. And to be honest, I was not sure that I could walk in their shoes. They were proven leaders, directors, professors, and doctors. I was not sure if I would measure up or even be considered eligible. But they thought I had a good chance.

I began reading more about it. I thought about it as a new opportunity to reach more people and open their hearts and minds. At the same time, it would teach me to be a better leader who could inspire others, influence legislation, and help improve the lives of many. I also knew it was not going to be easy. I was nervous and at the same time determined. Advocacy was my calling, and this opportunity was worth working for.

> **About the Fellowship**
>
> Joseph P. Kennedy Jr. was another of Mrs. Shriver's siblings. He died during World War II. The foundation bearing his name has supported the creation of programs to benefit people with intellectual disabilities, their families, and their communities. The fellowship is a one-year, full-time program the foundation sponsors to develop strong leaders in advocacy.

I exercised some diligence in preparing my application and sought recommendations from several people who knew me and my life goals. One was Dr. Ralph Shrader, who was then the CEO of Booz Allen Hamilton. I had worked for his company for almost twenty years, and he knew me well. In his letter of recommendation, he wrote, "[David] hopes he can influence the private sector to hire more people like him—a hope and commitment that I share with David."[6]

I asked former fellow Dr. Karen Summar for a letter, too. She wrote, "[David's] presence in the office made a tremendous statement about the value that people with disabilities bring to the workplace. David is a seasoned leader as a self-advocate for those with disabilities."[7]

"David has become a vocal champion for a fully inclusive society," wrote Representative McMorris Rodgers. "It is my hope that my son Cole, who has that extra twenty-first chromosome, will grow up to be just like

David. I cannot think of a more deserving and qualified advocate in action than David Egan."[8]

In my application, I highlighted my unique perspective, writing, "I strongly believe that self-advocates need to be directly involved in the issues that relate to their lives. I want to speak on behalf of many children and adults with intellectual disabilities. My goal is to promote awareness that we *are capable people*."

I cited many federal programs that directly affect people with disabilities. I pointed out that "having someone who has an *inside* understanding of what it means to have Down syndrome and an intellectual disability is critical." I continued,

> The Kennedy fellowship is stronger with someone who knows the issues from life experiences. I might not be the best guy to balance the budget or write a strategic plan, but I am the fellow that wants to be fully engaged in setting the priorities, the engagement with Congress, the business and nonprofit community.

I said that I had already been deeply involved with advocacy work but it had never been a full-time pursuit. I also wrote, "Those of us with intellectual disabilities want to be directly involved in issues that are about us; we do not want to be hidden from society, we do not want pity, but an opportunity to succeed. We want to be a part of that community that fights for and cares about us."

I finished strong: "I want to be the voice that speaks for us and ignites the dreams that belong to all of us. I want to bring unique insights that will enable the legislators to better understand the issues and foster medical, cognitive, and behavior research."[9]

A NEW FELLOW, A HISTORIC FIRST

My application and the help of the people who endorsed me paid off. In 2015, I learned that I had been chosen to be a Joseph P. Kennedy Jr. Public Policy Fellow, the first with an intellectual disability. My acceptance letter from the foundation's executive director, Steven Eidelman, said it all. "We are excited about the opportunities you will be creating for others, and for learning which you have as part of this effort," he wrote.[10]

Everyone was happy for me. My employer at that time was CBRE, and they were willing to support me. They offered me leave without pay and assurances of going back to my job at the completion of the fellowship. They were so proud of me that they wrote about me on their website.

Working on Capitol Hill was an honor and a privilege. It offered me the opportunity to learn about public policy, disability advocacy, and the political process.

My fellowship consisted of two assignments of about six months each. My first six months were with the Ways and Means Social Security Subcommittee of the U.S. House of Representatives. The second part of my fellowship was with the National Down Syndrome Society (NDSS) Public Policy Center.

My first day on the job with the subcommittee was scheduled for February 17, but it snowed so much the federal government in Washington closed down. It opened the next day, but the deep snow and cold weather still made my commute on the Metro slow and balky. In contrast with the cold weather, the staff was warm, welcome, and inclusive.

I learned that one of the subcommittee's roles is to make recommendations on Social Security benefits and support to people

My Goal: Inclusion

My biggest goal for my time in the fellowship was to help open doors for people with intellectual disabilities, showing their abilities and allowing them to contribute and achieve more. Employment helps give independence and dignity to people with disabilities. It also contributes to the betterment of all of society. The power of inclusion is evident when it helps overcome adversity and uncovers special gifts.

Talking Things Through

One man who stood out to me was Ted McCann, the staff director of the Social Security Subcommittee. Throughout my time on the Hill, he had an open-door policy for me and always took time in his busy schedule to talk things through. He helped with networking and building various coalitions. I love to build alliances and bring people together. Ted gave me opportunities to do both.

with disabilities. That was a good fit for me. The subcommittee reports to the Ways and Means Committee, which at that time was chaired by Representative Paul Ryan of Wisconsin. My first event as a staff member was a meet-and-greet with the people I would be working with daily. We met in a large conference room with heavy chairs, dim chandeliers, big windows with heavy curtains, and pictures of famous people on the walls. The setting was not new to me. I had been on Capitol Hill quite a few times advocating for people with disabilities with NDSS and Special Olympics, but this meeting was different.

I felt some nervousness, mixed with excitement. Everyone in the room went over their ideas for making sure my year on the Hill would be tremendous. My biggest joy on that day was to find out that almost all of the staffers who worked for Representative Ryan were from Wisconsin. Moreover, some of them were from Madison, where I was born. We bonded quickly.

My job was to learn as much as I could about policy and legislation in Congress, and support the subcommittee to the best of my abilities. My dad helped me research who was who in Congress. We put together a folder with photos of the members and their committees. I also made a calendar that showed when to dress up in a suit and tie, and when it was okay to skip the jacket and tie. I took the Metro to work most days, but sometimes my dad drove me into town in his electric car.

LEARNING AMID CHALLENGES

Working on the subcommittee was hard in several ways. The pace was different, I didn't know my way around, the subject matter was new to me, and I had to learn not to speak up the way I had as an advocate. I handled each one, but it made the early going tough.

The pace and schedule were like nothing I had experienced. In my job as a clerk in a distribution center, I had a well-defined routine and knew exactly what to do every single day. The first thing I learned on Capitol Hill is that no two days are alike. It was hard. It was hectic, with frequent changes and last-minute demands. Staffers juggle multiple tasks and need to be ready for the unpredictable. It was intense, especially for someone who thrives on consistency and schedule.

Getting around was hard at first, too. The offices of the Social Security Subcommittee were in the basement of the Longworth House Office Building. (Congress meets in the Capitol. The senators and representatives have offices in huge buildings near the Capitol. Longworth is one of them.) We had no windows, and the space was small. Everyone was a little worried I would get lost in the seemingly endless corridors and basement passages of the House office buildings. There's even an underground train for staff and members of Congress that goes from one side of Capitol Hill to the other.

I loved it all and learned how to navigate the labyrinth quite well. I was proud when friends would visit the Hill, and I would use my staff badge to take them on the underground train. I had my badge and a staff e-mail address; I was legit and official. I truly belonged.

I had to learn a lot fast. I was tasked to learn as much as possible about Supplemental Security Income (SSI). It was a daunting assignment with many reading assignments. SSI is a complicated topic, and the materials were not written with ease of reading in mind. My intellectual disability means I learn things more slowly than most people, and I have a hard time grasping complex topics. Studying SSI was exactly the kind of thing that challenged me most.

One way I've learned to be an advocate for myself is knowing when to ask for help. This was one of those times. My parents helped me understand the major points. Soon after that, my coworkers Erich and Ted found it was better for them to work directly with me instead of assigning readings of legal documents. That worked great for me. I prefer action to sitting at a desk all day long. (That's one way my distribution center job suited me well.) They included me in meetings, and I attended interesting hearings. The staff that I worked with on Capitol Hill had never worked with someone like me. I think it was beneficial for all of us. As time passed, we discovered one another's gifts. We made the most of our interactions despite the ever-changing schedules and time constraints.

One of the first surprising things I learned was that I could not be an active voice for people with disabilities while working on the Social Security Subcommittee. As a fellow and staffer, I could not express my personal opinions and views when meeting with visitors. My job was not to advocate but to listen to needs expressed through other people's advocacy. That was a hard thing to adapt to. My role was to learn, understand, and influence behind the scenes. It gave me a valuable perspective. And throughout time, it made me a more effective listener. But I often wanted to speak up and share my opinions, just as I had done my entire life.

I realized something, however. Just by being there, I was making a point about employment of people with disabilities. Having a badge and an account as a staff member gave me unique opportunities for acknowledgment as a fully integrated employee. Just being in the hallways of Congress and walking in and out of the buildings as a staffer raised awareness of the issue of employment for people like me. Oftentimes people would ask me where I worked. These unplanned meetings gave me the chance to engage in conversations and have a direct personal impact. I was a reminder to those around me that people with intellectual disabilities do not have to hide. We are citizens who matter and vote.

FAMILIAR FACES AND A NEW RELATIONSHIP

After about six months, I started the other part of my fellowship, working for the NDSS Public Policy Center, also in Washington, DC. It was in a different part of town, but I learned the new route quickly. A bonus for me was that it was a nice long walk to and from the nearest Metro station every day.

I already knew the people and goals of NDSS, so I got off to a good start. NDSS's mission is to be the "leading human rights organization for all individuals with Down syndrome by advocating for federal, state, and local policies that positively impact people with Down syndrome across the country."[11] That was a perfect fit with my fellowship. I still couldn't directly speak as an advocate, but by helping with training and administrative duties, I was making it possible for the organization to do more.

My previous relationships at the NDSS had been friendships. This was a business relationship, and that took a little bit of adjustment. It didn't take long before I was collaborating easily with the team in Washington. I took on a variety of tasks that would help the center with its advocacy work, but the one I am proudest of was related to employment. NDSS has a program called DSWORKS that focuses on encouraging employment of people with Down syndrome. The goal is to increase the opportunities for people with Down syndrome to have jobs that are meaningful and in competitive employment settings.[12] It was not a surprise that I was asked to work on that program, as I have twenty years of experience in competitive employment. Employment is important and a big part of defining who we are as adults.

I was the perfect person to help develop a resource guide called "Valued, Able, and Ready to Work." It is for employers of people with Down syndrome and other developmental disabilities. NDSS describes the resource guide as follows:

> Since the Americans with Disabilities Act (ADA) became law in 1990, employing people with Down syndrome and other disabilities has been a realistic goal for all kinds of employers—corporations, small and local businesses, and government agencies. However, many barriers to employment for individuals with Down syndrome still exist. Individuals with Down syndrome can and do make valuable employees and are ready to work, but they often lack the opportunity. Furthermore, many

employers have expressed interest in hiring employees with Down syndrome but often lack the information and resources to support opportunities for employment. This guide is intended to educate employers on hiring people with Down syndrome by highlighting benefits, suggesting tips for success, identifying some challenges, sharing success stories, and providing resources.[13]

The people of NDSS and many others know that people with Down syndrome are able and eager to work. The problem is the lack of opportunities. Part of the challenge is that potential employers are uncertain about how to work with people with Down syndrome. By solving that problem, more opportunities will become available.

As a Joseph P. Kennedy Jr. Public Policy Fellow, I was honored to lead the team effort in writing the resource guide for employers.[14] I used my personal experience to cover how to match employer and employee, engage the individual, sustain success on the job, and overcome barriers. As in any population, job seekers with Down syndrome have a range of abilities and personalities. It is important to work out the best fit through internships, assessments, individualized training, and mentorship. The resource guide offers such tips for success as setting concrete goals, providing a routine, meeting regularly, fostering inclusion, being flexible, keeping an open mind, educating other staff, and having realistic expectations.

Not long after I completed work on the resource guide, my time with the NDSS Public Policy Center came to an end, and that marked the end of my fellowship. A year seemed too short. It had gone by quickly, and I did not want it to end. In fact, it truly did not end, because "once a fellow, always a fellow." I had hesitated and wondered if I could—if I should—aim for being a fellow. I took the chance, and with the support of many, before and during the fellowship, I had made it a success. Now that it was over, I could aspire to even more. What I learned would help me be a stronger leader and advocate for people with disabilities.

REPRESENTING SPECIAL OLYMPICS WORLDWIDE

As busy as I was with the fellowship, I had other important work to do at the same time. I had the honor and duty of being a Special Olympics Sargent Shriver International Global Messenger—and this overlapped with my fellowship. It was a role that evolved from advocacy and leadership training I received through the Special Olympics Athlete Leadership Program. The program builds on the confidence and courage you get through Special Olympics sports. Athletes who are inclined can take part in training and opportunities to speak, and making decisions. I had been involved for a few years when the International Global Messenger (IGM) role came my way.

It was a dream come true. My class of IGMs was made up of athletes from Austria, Botswana, Egypt, Indonesia, South Korea, Macau, the Netherlands, Panama, Thailand, and the United States. The three of us from the United States were from Nebraska, New Hampshire, and Virginia. We learned a lot, worked a lot, and enjoyed one another's personalities.

I realized how small the world really is and how alike we all were. I felt I wasn't alone as we spent hours together, talking, eating, laughing, and growing closer. We were making a difference, and we knew it. We've stayed in touch throughout the years.

One of our first tasks was leadership training and preparation for the 2015 Special Olympics World Games in Los Angeles. We would all go to that big international event. We would need to be ready for a busy schedule doing a variety of jobs. To start the preparation, we met in Washington, DC. Each of us was assigned a mentor. I was so lucky to work with David Thomason, who had been a dear friend for many years. David is vice president of advancement for Special Olympics Virginia. He had trained me as an IGM for Special Olympics Virginia. He and I had traveled together to Morocco for an international meeting of Special Olympics Athletes in 2010. We've been through all kinds of challenges and experiences together. I felt blessed to be paired with him.

For the World Games in Los Angeles, I had a second mentor, Roy Zeidman, senior vice president for Special Olympics Virginia. Roy and I connected quickly and shared a room while going to the IGM events together.

"REACH UP LA"

The World Games in Los Angeles was a thrill. I had been to other World Games, but this one was different. I felt that everything was ready for me, and I was ready for everything. I felt comfortable and experienced in my role as a leader and speaker. Actually, I felt more than comfortable. I was excited and eager to help spread the word of the power of Special Olympics sports and programs. My fellow IGMs were among the six thousand two hundred athletes competing at the Summer Games. As many as five hundred thousand spectators saw the events and competitions. The Games were set on an international stage—literally. The magical experience of the Opening Ceremony will stay with me forever.

The kickoff to the 2015 Games was held in the historic Los Angeles Memorial Coliseum. The great old coliseum had been the site of two Olympic Games. It was our turn now. We were about to show the world our skill, determination, and courage in twenty-five sports. And I would be speaking at the Opening Ceremony. I took the stage in front of tens of thousands of people sitting in the stands of the coliseum. Hundreds of thousands of people saw me on the ESPN broadcast. From my point of view, it was a sea of joyful faces, with thousands of athletes in the uniforms of their home countries, from Afghanistan to Zimbabwe. Roy remembered it like this:

> David was about to speak to over fifty thousand spectators at the LA Coliseum! After his remarks, the parade of athletes would begin. This would give us time, we thought, to go into the stands to visit with his family. David did his part and came off the stage right on time.
>
> As we entered the stands, something unusual occurred. People in the stands began to recognize David, and he found himself surrounded by well-wishers who wanted autographs and pictures!
>
> I found this phenomenon to be incredible; reality matching our aspirations. Exactly what we dream of for every athlete!
>
> David handled this in his usual manner and spoke to each person, and relished taking pictures with whoever asked. . . . I had to take on a new role at that moment and become David's bodyguard to move us along so he could return backstage for his next assignment.
>
> It was during those Games, those experiences with David, that I realized the true power of Special Olympics occurs when we collectively celebrate what makes us alike.[15]

Roy and I were amazed when we read the *Los Angeles Times* the next day and saw my name included in the article titled "Special Olympics Opening Ceremony Is Out of This World." Reporter Bill Plaschke described the ceremony and noted that President Barack Obama took part via video. President Obama praised us athletes by saying, "You represent the very best of the human spirit." Plaschke added, "Equally impressive was David Egan, a former Special Olympics swimmer who was the first person to take the stage and immediately began leading the crowd in cheers."[16]

Everywhere in Los Angeles, there were big banners with photos of Special Olympics athletes and the slogan of the Games, "Reach Up LA." The games were my chance to spread my wings and demonstrate that I could speak to a thousand or a few, in public and in private, in interactions with celebrities and news media, with fellow athletes, families, fans, and bystanders.

THE FUN DUTIES OF AN INTERNATIONAL GLOBAL MESSENGER

As IGMs, we had so much to do. A lot of it was speaking, but that wasn't all. I took part in a strategic planning summit involving leaders both with and without disabilities from throughout the world. I enjoyed the summit, especially getting to learn about other countries and meeting many interesting individuals.

I also had the privilege of awarding medals to athletes after their competitions. That was great,

Nine Days of Good News

For the duration of the Summer Games, we were not forgotten anymore. ESPN and other media interviewed and photographed us, and filmed, wrote, published, and broadcast stories about us. The amount of news coming from Los Angeles was steady and unfailingly optimistic. It was the best nine days of news anyone could have asked for.

We offered a new way of thinking about sports. We offered a new way of thinking about humanity. We celebrated people from all corners of the world. We thought of ourselves as winners, and the world roared in agreement. Each of us was a story of empowerment, positivity, joy, equality, and confidence.

to share the joy and accomplishment of my fellow athletes. I always feel a kinship with Special Olympics athletes because of my many years competing in swimming, basketball, and other sports. Each of us is unique, but we share our determination to show the world that we understand sports and can play according to the rules of the game and compete with vigor.

I got my chance to do some playing during the LA Games. Special Olympics holds demonstrations of its Unified Sports at its World Games. Remember, in Unified Sports, the teams are made up of people both with and without intellectual disabilities. They play together and learn about one another. At World Games, these "Unified Sports Experience" games often involve celebrities, members of the Special Olympics Board of Directors, and athletes like me. This time, it was basketball. I got to play with some famous NBA players, one of whom was "Doc" Rivers, head coach for the Los Angeles Clippers of the National Basketball Association (NBA).

As an NBA point guard, Rivers was known for his defense, a trait that has carried over into his coaching. It was special for me to meet him, as I am also a point guard when I play basketball. I always wanted to compete in the World Games and never had the chance. But here in Los Angeles, I had the chance to play with legends of basketball in a unified game. It was almost surreal. Jalen Rose was on my team, and Dikembe Mutombo was one of the referees. After the game (my team won), photographers and news crews swarmed us. Interviewers asked us for our thoughts and to comment on the incredible experience. I came home with a gold medal and a memory to last me a lifetime.

CLOSING WORDS

Near the end of the Summer Games there was a celebration for the families who had come to Los Angeles with the Special Olympics athletes. There were celebrities; government officials; Special Olympics staff; and, of course, mothers, fathers, sisters, brothers, and other proud relatives.

I had the chance to speak there, too. It was my chance to thank my family in front of everyone. I wanted to let them know how much they have helped me become the athlete and advocate I have become. At the same time, I wanted to thank Special Olympics families for doing the same for their athletes.

"The world is small today," I said. "There are no barriers, and we become one big family when we meet at Special Olympics World Games. At World Games, the athletes are the stars and the champions that we celebrate; however, without you, the families, there would be no stars and no champions."

After that, there were many embraces, hugs, and tears of joy. The sun was setting. The crowd was calm and refreshed by an afternoon of music, food, and friendship. Everyone went home with hearts full of joy.

The 2015 Special Olympics Summer Games ended soon thereafter with a burst of joy, with music, dancing, and a sense of accomplishment. I spoke at the Closing Ceremony, sending off athletes, families, and friends after nine incredible days.

FINDING A NEW OPPORTUNITY IN AUSTRIA

I returned from Los Angeles and got back to work. I continued my role as an IGM. In early 2017, it was time for the next big international event, the Special Olympics World Winter Games in Austria. The events were spread throughout the city of Graz and the mountainous areas of Schladming-

Rohrmoos and Ramsau. The Winter Games draw smaller numbers of competing athletes compared with the Summer Games, but the welcoming spirit of togetherness is the same.

We twelve IGMs were there as a team. It was like a reunion. I spoke at a media reception, introducing myself as an "American from Vienna." Since the capital of Austria is Vienna, I added, "Vienna, *Virginia*, a small town close to Washington, DC." I am always on the lookout for a quip.

I had a message prepared for the media that I hoped they would pass along to their readers and viewers in their home countries: "By accepting who we are, by accepting others who may be different, and then discovering what we have in common, we are the heartbeat for the world. By telling our stories in every town, on every street, we let the people know that we have dreams, we have rights, and we have lives that matter."

Being out among people you know and those you don't know is part of finding and shaping opportunities. I found that out once more at the Winter Games in Austria. With so many leaders of all kinds and from so many countries, Special Olympics makes sure that those great minds get together. There are meetings on education, government, healthcare, and employment. That was clearly something I knew more than a little bit about.

I listened carefully. When I started work as a clerk in a mail room, it was a satisfying moment. It felt like a real accomplishment, and it was. I had earned a good job with benefits after applying and interviewing like everyone else does. Throughout the years, my ambitions grew as I mastered the job and became comfortable in it. In the incredible year of 2015, opportunities I hadn't even considered became mine to try for. And in 2017, my hard work and experience paid off with a job where advocacy is a daily pursuit.

Working in SourceAmerica's Government Affairs department was a perfect fit. SourceAmerica's mission aligns with my goals in advocacy, helping people with disabilities find meaningful work by removing barriers to their opportunities. People at SourceAmerica embrace the mission as much as I do.

Shane Kanady is SourceAmerica's vice president of Workforce Development and has worked with me for a couple of years now. He had this to say about me:

> I have never met someone as determined to change the world as David. His persistence and passion are infectious. Like many of us, he sets his sights very high. But, unlike most, he has the ability to bring people together in support of his vision. David is a leader, and I am fortunate to be his coworker and friend.[17]

My time in the fellowship on Capitol Hill opened my eyes. I saw how lawmaking really works. It's not as simple as delivering a speech and having votes go your way. The speech is sometimes the last step of a process that involves months or years of work, dozens or hundreds of meetings, and the steady evolution of a set of words that define your goal. No one does it alone because no one can. Every person who joins the process contributes. I think I added a lot to the things I worked on, on Capitol Hill, at NDSS, and at Special Olympics. Just by being part of the process, I opened people's eyes to the value of different ways of thinking. Future meetings, debates, policies, and laws might be affected in some small way by the fact that I had been there. And maybe my having been there will inspire someone else to dare make their dreams come true, too.

8

A RESEARCH PARTICIPANT

The Upside of Down

> David Egan is a brilliant, eloquent, charismatic leader who not
> only talks the talk, but also walks the walk. He is an excep-
> tional role model not just for people with Down syndrome,
> but for anyone wanting to lead his or her best life. His fun
> road trips with his father and brother to take part in longi-
> tudinal studies shows how quick and rewarding research can
> be, and these are just one more way that David is having a
> profound impact on the lives of people worldwide. My hope
> is that individuals will feel empowered to do more at home,
> at school, in the workplace, in their communities, and, of
> course, with research.
>
> —Michelle Whitten, cofounder and executive director of
> the Global Down Syndrome Foundation[1]

Not long ago, I had the chance to speak in front of a meeting of scientists and researchers at one of the top research centers in the world,
the U.S. National Institutes of Health (NIH). I was addressing an advisory
group that helps decide the focus of research at the National Institute of
Child Health and Human Development (NICHD).

You might wonder what I could tell this knowledgeable and influential group. I'm not a researcher. I know a bit about science, sure, but I'm
more of a talker and an athlete than a scientist.

Well, it turns out, there was a lot for me to say. I'm a research participant and a man with Down syndrome. Those are two things that make
me important to researchers. I don't think a lot of research subjects get to
talk to the people who steer funding for their research, but I did. And I
made the most of it.

"There are more and more adults with Down syndrome who are living longer, and our aging population is at a very high risk of being affected by depression and Alzheimer's disease," I said. "While we have made some progress in the acceptance of people with intellectual disabilities and our quality of life has greatly improved, we still have no answers on preventing or curing heart defects, Alzheimer's, and other diseases."[2]

This advisory group was chock full of distinguished researchers from universities and children's hospitals throughout the United States. And I had their attention.

"I am here today to urge you to continue to support Down syndrome research," I told them.

> I hope the medical and research community will find studying Down syndrome to be exciting and interesting. I hope that they will find out that the extra chromosome will unlock discoveries of how the brain works, how children develop language, cognitive, and social skills. Research on Down syndrome could make it easier to understand diseases that affect us all.

This was January 2018, and I had learned firsthand about some of this. I had been poked with needles and asked questions that tested my memory. Little bits of my skin were in study samples under microscopes. People in lab coats had examined my brain with sophisticated scanning machines. I knew that the research studies I took part in were small but important. I had a stake in what that advisory council thought about Down syndrome research. As you will see, research is on my mind a lot because of what could await me in future years.

I LOVE RESEARCH

Research on the things that make up human life is fascinating to me—how we grow, think, and dream, and how we learn, communicate, and learn to judge, choose, and decide. What motivates us? How do we learn to overcome challenges and

---

I Help Make Magic Happen

My brother Marc has explained to me that some of the biggest discoveries in biology have come from seeing how different people's bodies work. Down syndrome makes my body work a little differently from most people's bodies. Thus, studying me lets researchers discover what's the same and what's different about me and people who don't have three twenty-first chromosomes. It's complex, but that's where the magic happens and discoveries are made.

disabilities? All of this interests me. Research that leads to new discoveries helps us strive for better lives, whether we have disabilities or not. I've been part of research studies my entire life, starting with at the University of Wisconsin when I was young. I've been part of studies at the NIH near Washington, DC. I am still involved with studies, but not just as a subject of research.

As you saw earlier, I am an advocate for further research on people like me. Maybe one day, new research results will translate into benefits that improve my life and the lives of others both with and without disabilities.

That doesn't mean I am asking scientists to change me. I am comfortable with who I am. When I was ten, I was at the hospital to have my tonsils taken out. I was sitting in the waiting room and trying to understand what tonsils were when I started wondering about Down syndrome. My mom had tried to explain it to me, but I still didn't quite get it at that age.

What was DNA? What did it mean to have three twenty-first chromosomes? Isn't three of something better than just two? And what are chromosomes, anyway?

I began to think that if the doctors could remove my tonsils, maybe they could remove my Down syndrome, too. Maybe at the same time? When I was sitting in the hospital bed about to go under anesthesia, I mustered up the courage and asked, "Are you going to remove this Down syndrome thing, too?"

There was an awkward pause in the room. The doctors and my mother huddled around me. My mother is a courageous woman who has always helped explain anything I have ever asked her with the honest truth. She did not miss a beat.

"Down syndrome will stay with you all your life," she said, "but it will not stop you from having dreams and being successful."

She was right, Down syndrome does not define me. Since that day, I have looked at my Down syndrome differently.

DISABILITY DOES NOT MEAN NO ABILITY

If you think about the word *disability*, you will see that it means something that most people are "able" to do but some cannot for some reason. People who have a physical disability may not be able to walk because of a problem with their legs. People who have hearing disabilities have some kind of problem with their ears. I have an intellectual disability, and that means I have difficulty learning new things and understanding complex topics. But people with physical disabilities get around with the help of canes, crutches, wheelchairs, motorized chairs, and special vans. People who are deaf or hard of hearing use sign language, lip-reading, hearing aids, closed captioning, and plain old handwriting to communicate. And I learn by taking it slow, breaking things into smaller pieces, practicing a lot, and, yes, thinking a lot. So my friends in wheelchairs get to places on time, my deaf friends follow movies and laugh with me, and I understand how chromosomes work and make me different from most other people.

So yes, people with disabilities need help from others in some ways. But I think we can also help others by showing that our abilities are what truly matter in our lives. When we overcome hurdles on our journey, we provide an example to others who don't have significant disabilities. My brother Marc says that I taught him how to be compassionate and open to seeing that differences can unify us in understanding. He is a manager and now has an uncanny skill of focusing on the positive abilities of his teammates and not their weaknesses. He learned that as he grew up with me as his older brother. He saw me as a person with skills and challenges, but he also saw that my challenges didn't stop me from achieving what I really wanted to achieve.

I have challenges, and I need help—but who doesn't? No one is perfect. And everyone faces challenges. We all count on others at times. And you don't need research to see that being able to count on one another makes us stronger, not weaker.

Being part of this research means I got to meet and talk to the scientists doing the research. I was always asking questions when I was little, and my curiosity and interest in science got a boost from being surrounded by researchers. My parents were PhD students in Madison, Wisconsin, and most of their friends were graduate students and professors at the University of Wisconsin.

My early exposure to scientists was fun. I didn't understand it then, but I am proud that I was a subject of research by people who were interested in every aspect of my development. My parents had friends in the medical and nursing school at the University of Wisconsin, so I was pretty well known to nursing professors and medical interns.

ONE BENEFIT OF HAVING ACADEMICS AS PARENTS

My first involvement in research began when I was about ten months old. Scientists from nearby Waisman Research Center[3] at the University of Wisconsin were studying human development, developmental disabilities, and neurodegenerative diseases. A little guy like me with Down syndrome was a perfect test subject, plus I was right in the neighborhood.

Two researchers became interested in tracking my motor skills, observing how well and how quickly I learned to use my small and large muscles as I developed. Dr. Ana Doodlah and her student, Rita Holstein, would visit me at our home once a month to check and document my progress with notes and videos.

Rita wrote to me to share her memories of those sessions. She had been particularly interested in seeing how I developed my ability to pick up things with my fingers. When she compared my skills to other kids my age, my scores were disappointing. But she knew I was learning. She saw that I learned all of the finger skills that the average child learns. Her insight was that the pace of my learning didn't predict how much I would eventually learn.

> **Let's Study This**
>
> Here's another thing that humans often do that I wish someone *could* cure. Having a disability in one part of your life doesn't mean other parts of your life are affected. But people think that is true. People see someone in a wheelchair, let's say, and think they are less able in ways that have nothing to do with walking. People may underestimate people who cannot see or hear well, even though their issues with their eyes or ears may have nothing to do with their ability to learn. I have challenges with learning facts and mastering ideas, but I excel in other ways. I love jokes and wordplay. I am a great swimmer and softball player. I am calm in front of big crowds, and I have a gift for reaching people through my public speaking. And I have no trouble understanding people's feelings and emotions.

"The body and mind he was born with, in addition to the fantastic stimulation and support he received from his parents and family, would be the critical factors in determining what he could accomplish," she wrote.[4]

Many years passed before I saw her again. And when we did meet, another thing clicked for her.

"A diagnosis for any child need not limit the lengths that the individual may attain," she wrote. "David, as a young adult, has accomplished more than most people his age, and there is no limit to what he may accomplish and contribute in the future."[5]

As an adult, I've watched the monthly videos they took during our sessions. I was funny, always smiling and happy to pose for the camera. (Some things never change.) I loved being the center of attention and wanted to impress everyone with all that I had. But at that time, I did not have much stamina to keep going, just like many other babies with Down syndrome. I had trouble using my big muscles together to move forward. It took a long time for me to learn to crawl. My dad and mom would put a pillow under my tummy to lean me forward a little so I would move forward, but I kept going backward. In the videos, it looks like I was trying to be an airplane with my arms and legs all sticking out like wings and rudders. I moved back and forth like a rocking chair going nowhere fast.

But I loved balls, and I always wanted to play with them. I talked earlier about our regular game: my dad would put balls near me and just out of reach to motivate me to crawl and press forward. Every time I got close, Dad would move the ball a little farther away until he felt I had earned some playtime. Seeing those balls and wanting to reach out and grab them helped me dig deeper and try harder. My mom and dad understood that I was just like other kids in that way, and they simply used something I wanted as a tool to bring out the best in me. By tweaking what motivated me, my parents led me patiently from crawling to the literal baby steps that made me a walker by eighteen months and on to other things that have helped me thrive.

> ### Learning to Crawl
>
> I had a hard time putting it all together to learn to crawl. People say you need to learn to crawl before you can run, but I needed to learn basic muscle movements before I could crawl. I wish my parents could have seen the future me: a swimmer who would win countless Special Olympics races by coordinating every muscle of my body, along with the rhythm of breathing. When I was struggling so hard to inch forward, it would have been great for them to see just one of the gold medals I have in my room now.

At the University of Wisconsin medical and nursing school, I was often asked if students could listen to my heart. You may remember I was born with a heart defect called ventricular septal defect (VSD), a hole between the two big chambers of the heart. It is the most common type of heart issue present at birth among babies, and many babies with Down syndrome are born with it. VSD allows blood from the left chamber to leak into the right chamber, and that's not good.[6] I grew out of it, but I still have my heart checked every three years. So far so good!

I HELP BRIGHTEN UP A TEXTBOOK

In one way, VSD led to something very good: It got photos of me included in a nursing textbook. (As you can see, I like to see the upside of Down syndrome.) Professor Mecca Cranley knew my mother, who was a program evaluator for the Nurse Practitioner's University Program. My mother shared photos of me with Professor Cranley as she revised her *Obstetrics Nursing* textbook to its eighth edition.[7] For this version, she wanted to feature happier faces and stress the importance of family. Most textbooks with pictures of children with Down syndrome did not show them as beautiful, happy babies.

Since I was both beautiful and happy (in my mother's opinion, at least), the revised textbook included photos of me. I was featured in a chapter about genetics and genetic counseling. There I am again, in the chapter on "Psychosocial Adaptation of the Childbearing Family." Professor Cranley used photos of me as a baby and also a picture from when I was older, posing with my baby sister Teresa, who is three years younger than me. There was a great photo of four generations of my family, me included, highlighting the importance of family support to new parents. The caption for that picture says family "provides role models, affection, and a sense of continuity over generations."[8] That is really true. I am glad to be part of a generation that embraced me as part of the family.

MY GENERATION MARKED A TURNING POINT

My own generation is the one when people with Down syndrome began to break free from the institutions that had unintentionally but deeply limited our potential.

Even before I was born, there were outcries in the 1960s to close the institutions that were supposedly *treating* (more like hiding) individuals with intellectual and developmental disabilities. Think about this: Every human being needs love, experiences, and challenges when they are growing up. Anyone raised in the numbing environment of an institution would fall behind peers raised in a family setting. The institutions denied attention, help, and enriching experiences, and even medical care, to the people who needed it most. It created a cycle of low achievement that fed low expectations. When you don't expect much, you don't push for much. And that cycle continues.

Down syndrome is the most common genetic cause of intellectual and developmental disabilities. Even so, we were excluded from research that could improve our health and quality of life. (And we were usually excluded from society in general.) Funding for Down syndrome research was scarce, and few researchers were seeking grants to study Down syndrome. Famously, Robert Kennedy visited the Willowbrook State School on Staten Island, which was later exposed by journalist Geraldo Rivera as having horrendous conditions.[9] It is thanks to the journalists, lawmakers, and public pressure that many of these institutions were closed down. They were replaced with expanded special education programs in public schools, housing options in communities, and better health care for individuals with disabilities. These things together meant people with disabilities could live longer, healthier, happier lives in the communities that make up our society.

Institutions Would Hold Anyone Back

I was one of the fortunate ones during this era in American society. Much as Steve Jobs and Bill Gates were born in the right place and right time for the personal computer and information technology revolution, I was born into a changing era. The institutions where individuals with Down syndrome had previously been hidden away were closing. In those human warehouses, most children like me were not exposed to learning and experiences that would help them succeed and thrive. So when people with Down syndrome were in institutions, they didn't get the things they needed to grow their minds and bodies. They didn't thrive because they had no chance to.

Instead of being isolated, I was the center of attention for a loving, dedicated group of researchers and parents who would not leave any stone unturned to find the best path forward for me. I think I was actually more fortunate than Steve Jobs and Bill Gates, in fact. Their parents frowned when they dropped out of college, but Jobs and Gates had not been told by society that they would never amount to anything. My parents knew that the world had low expectations for people like me, but they knew better.

When I was born, few people with Down syndrome lived to be older than twenty-five years of age. Today, we are living much longer. Research has given us a boost in our education and medical care. But there is still much work to do.

I am a *Star Trek* fan, and I love science fiction. I dare to dream and hope that the next generation of individuals with intellectual and developmental disabilities can "live long and prosper," as Science Officer Spock from *Star Trek* puts it. Spock also teaches us that the things that make us different are the same things that make us awesome. I believe that is true.

BACK TO WISCONSIN FOR A MEMORIAL AND A PANEL

I went back to the Waisman Research Center in 2002, when I was twenty-five. I visited the Early Childhood Program, where, to my surprise, one of my teachers, Becky Lewis, was still teaching. She was so happy to see me after all those years. She had a lively young spirit, and I was happy to see her, too. She was one of the few teachers left from our first inclusive class in 1979.

I visited the Waisman Research Center eleven years later, in 2013, but for the sad purpose of a memorial in honor of my teacher Becky. I was privileged to give the commendation speech and meet with alumni, parents, and students. Every time I set foot in the building, I get excited to hear about its work and growth. What started with twelve kids in one class is now a center with more than one hundred fifty kids and multiple classes. The growth of the center is one example of the progress that has been made in our country and society during the course of my life. We now have a better awareness of disability and childhood developmental needs. I am grateful for the wonderful beginnings I had there.

The 2013 visit was memorable because of the emotions I felt and the meaningful interactions I had. Meeting with and talking to researchers gives me a chance to make an impact and raise awareness. It says to the researchers, "Hey, here I am! I am one of the individuals your research is supporting." I think it inspires academic researchers when they can see that their work matters to real people. I love showing and telling how I live a full life, while at the same time reminding an audience that there's still room for improvement.

During that trip to Madison, I got another chance to tell my story. I was on a panel discussion called Reflections on Inclusion, put together by Elizabeth Hecht, a public policy specialist at the

A Mission I Admire

The organization that sponsored the panel discussion is dedicated to supporting the "full inclusion and self-determination of people with developmental disabilities and their families."[10] Elizabeth Hecht is a believer in inclusion. She works to bring together advocacy and lawmaking at the federal level. Her goal is to create opportunities for people with disabilities, and one important way to do that is to get funding for researchers in that field.

university's Center for Excellence in Developmental Disabilities. In her invitation to people to attend, Elizabeth wrote that the "current generation of self-advocates grew up expecting to work, contribute, and live in their communities. . . . Individuals with disabilities have the possibility for a far different experience today than in previous generations."[11] That was exciting to talk about because it meant that my family and I were pioneers in a way. I knew a bit about institutionalization, but this session really made it clear to me that my generation was doing something new.

My fellow panelists included another young adult with Down syndrome, Claire Bible, and a young man with autism, Jeremy Gilomen. We talked about growing up, going to school, making friends, trying to find jobs, and how we felt about our place in our communities. Each of us gave our opinions about what had helped us thrive and also what we still aspired to do in our lives.

Our audience was a group of researchers, so we got a chance to give them advice in person. I asked them to always remember that we people with disabilities matter in the real world, so including us makes their research more relevant to the entire community. The trip to Madison was making me feel motivated, inspired, and appreciated, and I wanted the researchers to feel the same way.

Research Is Like Life

I have a brilliant cousin, Nasri Nesnas, a tenured professor of biological chemistry at the Florida Institute of Technology. He explained to me how the research process takes on little slices of the world, studying them from varying angles before coming up with a theory to explain the little parts of these slices. Life goes on regardless of what happens in the lab, and it may seem like the scientific research and the real world are not necessarily connected. In a way, the gradual contributions that research and discovery make are like the long process of a person's life. Day by day, there are little changes with gradual but significant improvements or decline. Some days, maybe there are no changes. But when you look at a person during a span of multiple years, the changes can be big, especially considering the impact they may have on those around them. Every day is important, because every day makes up every week, and weeks make up months, and months make up years. It's a process that enables numerous interactions with people around us, as well as our environment. There is always something new we can learn and subsequently teach by sharing it with others.

DOING MY PART FOR RESEARCH

If I can do something to help researchers make progress, I am up for it. So, on that same trip to Madison in 2013, my dad and I volunteered to be part of another research project. This one involved stem-cell therapy, real cutting-edge stuff. Dr. Anita Bhattacharyya,[12] a senior scientist at the Waisman Center's Stem Cells and Developmental Disorders Lab, was studying how a particular part of the brain, the cerebral cortex, develops in people with disabilities like mine. That part of the brain is where we do most of our thinking and planning. It's the part that allows us to talk and listen, as well as write and read. In other words, it is the part most affected by an intellectual disability. Interested? You bet I was.

"Problems in any of the crucial steps in the formation of the cerebral cortex can lead to mental impairment," Dr. Bhattacharyya wrote. Her research focused on Down syndrome and Fragile X syndrome, two disabilities that relate to genes and human development. Down syndrome is caused by an extra twenty-first chromosome in the DNA. Fragile X syndrome is due to a single gene mutation.

Dr. Bhattacharyya was using a special kind of stem cell that can make many different kinds of other cells. They're the master stem cell, also called pluripotent stem cells. She used master stem cells that had either Fragile X or Down syndrome to study how the cerebral cortex grows in lab conditions outside the body.

She was looking for where things went wrong. It's like my brother Marc told me a long time ago: When you can see how things are different in my body, it tells you something about how things work in people without Down syndrome.

If Dr. Bhattacharyya's project could help us understand how development of the brain could go wrong, it might also lead the way to treatments to help it grow correctly. And my dad and I could help make that happen.

Getting the stem cells to study meant getting blood and skin samples from research subjects, in this case, my dad and me. The research involved people with and without developmental disabilities. As a result, they needed samples from people with Down syndrome or Fragile X syndrome and those without. And since it also involved genetic differences, they needed cells from related people of the same sex.

My dad and I were perfect subjects. His cells would be the "control" set, and mine would be the "variable" set. When the researchers get the stem cells to turn into brain cells, they can see how my cells with Down syndrome behaved differently.

Getting the blood sample involved getting poked so my blood would flow into the collecting tube. The skin sample involved a biopsy, which is cutting out a tiny chunk of my skin to do its part for science.

I was happy and thankful that my dad was willing to do it with me. He was more nervous than I was during the skin biopsy procedure.

He asked the doctor, "Does it hurt?"

The doctor said, "No."

So my dad said, "Have you ever had a skin biopsy?"

The doctor, smiling coyly, said, "No. But I am the best doctor for biopsies."

We had a good laugh, but in the end it did kind of hurt to do the biopsy. As I said, I am happy to do what I have to do to help research, even if it hurts a little.

INTEREST IN RESEARCH RUNS IN THE FAMILY

I am lucky to have a family that believes in research and is enthusiastic about teaming up with me on these medical research adventures. My brother Marc is also my champion. He offered to be my partner in a research effort that will take four years to complete. We signed up for the Neurodegeneration in Aging Down Syndrome (NIAD) study at the University of Pittsburgh. It's being run by Dr. Benjamin Handen and Dr. Peter Bulova, and is funded by NIH.

NIH is the leading research entity in the United States for health-related studies. Research done through NIH suggests the extra chromosome in people with Down syndrome may hold clues for treatments and even cures for many diseases.

The NIAD study is based on the fact that individuals with Down syndrome have a higher risk of developing Alzheimer's

NIH's Down Syndrome Research Plan

In 2011, NIH joined with U.S. and international organizations interested in Down syndrome to form the Down Syndrome Consortium. The goal was to encourage the exchange of information about Down syndrome research, support, and care among the groups in the consortium. The consortium meets to discuss research findings and progress toward achieving goals set out by NIH. Those goals were set after consulting with national organizations and agencies interested in Down syndrome. Those organizations helped develop the first NIH-wide research plan on Down syndrome.

disease than most other people. According to the study's synopsis, that is likely because "protein deposits associated with these conditions are made by a gene on the twenty-first chromosome. . . . Since individuals with Down syndrome have an extra twenty-first chromosome, they have an increased risk of developing these deposits, which can start happening years before symptoms of memory loss appear."[13]

The NIAD study team in Pittsburgh is part of a larger research team working with others in Wisconsin and Cambridge in the United Kingdom. I am one of as many as two hundred people with Down syndrome taking part in the study.

Researchers will be studying us during an extended period of time to see if they can spot early signs of Alzheimer's disease. If they can do that, they might be able to develop new ways of testing for the disease. This study will be the largest and most comprehensive effort to do this type of analysis for individuals with Down's syndrome. My brother and I will be letting scientists look into our brains with sophisticated scanning equipment. Researchers will put a compound into our blood so that when they scan, they can see some telltale signs that could relate to Alzheimer's disease. They will also test our cognitive capabilities. We will make four two-day visits during the four-year span of the study.[14] My brother stands as the control for me in the experiment, so he has to do the same tests I do.

A WITNESS TO DEMENTIA

My grandfather and grandmother on my father's side had dementia at the end of their lives. I watched them go through the different phases, losing the most precious possession of their minds—their personalities—as they also lost their independence. The memory has stuck with me. I never knew all of that could come with having Down syndrome. I have prided myself on being as independent as possible, as my parents have taught me to be. Losing independence and personality through dementia is a scary thought.

The experience of seeing my dad's parents decline made me want to be part of the NIAD study. I also think part of me is scared about how fast aging happens with Down syndrome. I worry that Alzheimer's might be part of my future after so many years of trying to grow and overcome adversity. It would be an insurmountable roadblock cast in front of me.

When I was with the researchers at Madison, Wisconsin, when I was very little, everything was about growth and potential. Dementia would be the opposite of that. The thought of having everything I have worked for ripped away from me makes me very sad. This is why I have to have faith—and a lot of hope—that this research will help. I think about it often. I don't want the next generation to have to face it, too. I will add one tiny set of statistics to this study, but my set may show some crucial difference that researchers can follow to a treatment. I hope with all my heart that I and my fellow adults with Down syndrome can play a role in ending Alzheimer's disease for everyone who faces it.

STARTING THE STUDY IN PITTSBURGH

Marc drove my mother and me to Pittsburgh for our initial procedures and meetings in June of 2018. The research coordinator, Cathy Wolfe, had arranged lodging for us close to their offices at the University of Pittsburgh Hospital. Of course, we missed our turn off the Pittsburgh Turnpike on the way there and got an impromptu tour of the city.

After settling in, we spent the evening strolling the streets of the college downtown area. We were told to stop by Primanti Bros. restaurant for a classic Pittsburger, which is a specialty hamburger topped with delicious coleslaw and French fries tucked inside a huge bun. Unfortunately, we could not enjoy a beer with the burger because we had to be on our A game for the lab and cognitive tests the next day. Plus, Marc was put off by all the Pittsburgh Penguins hockey players featured on the wall next to where we were eating. Even though our hometown team, the Washington Capitals, had

A Central Place for Research Data

An important Down syndrome conference was held in 2010, at NIH, a result of the Global Down Syndrome Foundation's congressional advocacy. The focus was registry, biobanks, and databases. As a result of that conference, NICHD created a Down syndrome consortium and a Down syndrome health registry that enables researchers to learn more about the condition from those who live with it. The Down Syndrome Registry DS-Connect® aims to learn more about the health of those with Down syndrome and accelerate research that benefits people with the condition. DS-Connect® is part of that research community, encouraging families to share their information. Gathering research data in a single place and providing it for free could encourage more researchers to investigate Down syndrome. The database and the research that will follow will help us all improve the quality of our lives.

just clinched the Stanley Cup, the days of battling our archnemesis, the Penguins, were still far from over.

The next morning, we headed to the office, where the researchers, Dr. Handen and Dr. Bulova, met us. They gave us a thorough review of the study and background information on why Down syndrome could help in the journey to Alzheimer's treatments.

Then it was time for testing to begin. The psychologist who tested my cognitive ability asked me a bunch of questions to test my memory. She was very nice, and I wanted to joke with her. She kept having me memorize phone numbers or other random numbers in different scenarios. I finally asked her if I could just memorize her phone number and be done with it. She had a good laugh.

My intellectual disability makes learning harder, and that's something they tested. Sometimes I get confused trying to follow directions if they're a bit complicated. I sometimes try to take the easy way out with a simple answer, to avoid admitting I don't understand. I think I followed all the test directions, but I am not sure how I did or how my answers helped study Alzheimer's disease. The psychologist who tested me and Dr. Handen told me that some people spend more than three hours taking the test. I must have done somewhat well, as I completed all the tests in about an hour.

The next morning, Marc and I had more tests, some of which involved time in an MRI machine. That day turned out to be the toughest so far. I awoke feeling slightly ill from something I had eaten on the trip to Pittsburgh. My brother did not help the situation. The thought of being trapped inside the tunnel of the MRI

Looking at Me from Just One Perspective

My mother told me they were testing me to set a baseline for my memory, comprehension, and intelligence—basically, my IQ. They measured those narrow parts of me, but they have not yet tested my emotional intelligence, my intuition, my ability to read people, and my ability to socialize and build networks. They have measured my thinking skills, my cognitive brain, and not the other things that make up my personality. I've never liked that people often think that those with Down syndrome are so unlike them because of our intellectual disability. The parts of our brains that inspire us to love, to have friends, to want to learn and grow, to make people laugh— they are pretty much the same as everyone else's. We're more alike than different in so many ways. But the researchers wanted to focus on the differences. So, IQ and memory it is! For now.

machine, hearing the constant bang-bang-bang of the scanner, unsettled Marc because he hates tight spaces.

When I was getting ready for the MRI, they put me in a kind of strait-jacket thing that would keep me still if I fell asleep. My brother told the technicians that I would likely fall asleep, and if I fell asleep, I might move somehow and ruin the test. Well, I didn't fall asleep. They put plugs in my ears to soften the noise, but the plugs fell out. I couldn't move my hands, so I couldn't put them back in. The magnets were banging like a techno club—a club I did not want to be in. No trap or dubstep music for me. I wanted out. Things were off to a bad start as far as I was concerned. Thankfully, the PET machine was better. I didn't have to slide into a tunnel, like the MRI machine. It was like a big doughnut around my head. You could even have another person in the room with you. The nurses and technicians were fantastic and explained everything.

Our day as guinea pigs finally ended. We went to a Pittsburgh Pirates baseball game to celebrate going from research subjects to regular people again. We bought tickets and walked into the stadium with smiles on our faces. Finally, we could relax, have those beers, and watch a game. We could see the river that flows through the heart of Pittsburgh. It felt good. And it felt good to be done with the two days of tests. It was our way to make a small contribution to the fight against Alzheimer's.

> **Two Reasons to Be Excited**
>
> INCLUDE is a big program. It took the Global Down Syndrome Foundation and our community almost ten years to advocate for it. It involves twenty institutes and centers at NIH, one of which is the Eunice Kennedy Shriver National Institute of Child Health and Human Development—NICHD. It has provided $56 million in new Down syndrome funding in two years, with more planned in the future. I am excited about the project because it's another example of research involving people with Down syndrome. I am also pleased that the lead institute is named for Eunice Kennedy Shriver, the founder of Special Olympics.

A BIG CHANGE IN DOWN SYNDROME RESEARCH

It turns out that the project in Pittsburgh is part of a much bigger project focusing on Down syndrome and how its unique traits can help scientists understand more about people in general. The project is called INCLUDE, and it kicked off in June 2018. INCLUDE stands for INvestigation of Co-occurring conditions across the Lifespan to Understand Down syndromE. That's a nice play on words. Finally, research that is focusing on "understanding Down syndrome" and its nickname reminds people about inclusion. The project is meant to study "co-occurring conditions," which are diseases or disorders that often affect people with Down syndrome. Alzheimer's disease is one of them, of course. Autism, cataracts, celiac disease, diabetes, and congenital heart disease (like the hole in my heart I was born with) are other examples.

The co-occurring conditions and diseases are things that affect all kinds of people. But this project "aims to understand critical health and quality-of-life needs for individuals with Down syndrome." It is basic science research that could make "discoveries that improve the health, well-being, and neurodevelopment of individuals with Down syndrome." The project will look at how often people with Down syndrome get these common diseases and also how deeply the diseases affect us. Researchers will compare that information with the general population of people who don't have Down syndrome.[15]

MY HERO, EUNICE KENNEDY SHRIVER

My relationship with NIH and their initiatives started because of a personal hero of mine, Eunice Kennedy Shriver. In her life, she took on society's misconceptions about people with intellectual disabilities. From major new laws in Congress to the founding of Special Olympics, her powerful and persuasive nature made the United States, and the world, a more welcoming place. She was driven to do such ambitious things because she saw how her sister Rosemary was treated. Rosemary, like me, had an intellectual disability.

I am so grateful for Mrs. Shriver's vision, leadership, and relentless efforts to give Rosemary and everyone with a disability a chance to have a life like everyone else's. I dare to say that I was one of her dear friends before she died in 2009. I met her and her husband, Sargent Shriver, when I was young. My friendship with her lives on through the rest of her family, who are great advocates and friends for me and many others throughout the world.

In 2008, I was honored to be invited to a ceremony that honored the dedication and power for good that Mrs. Shriver brought to the world. In a ceremony attended by top researchers, famous dignitaries, and members of Congress, her name was added to two major parts of NIH. On that day, the Eunice Kennedy Shriver National Institute of Child Health and Human Development—NICHD—was christened. At the same time, NIH's Mental Retardation and Developmental Disabilities Research Centers Program was renamed the Eunice Kennedy Shriver Intellectual and Developmental Disabilities Research Centers Program. That change was big because it also removed the words *mental retardation* from the name and replaced them with *intellectual disability.*

The event took place on the NIH campus in Maryland. My father, mother, and I were excited to witness this historic moment, and we got there early. It felt as if a new era was just beginning. The Natcher Auditorium got fuller and fuller with famous, brilliant, and powerful people. Mrs. Shriver was there, too, with the Kennedy and Shriver families nearby. She was loved and honored by all those people, and I was proud to be among them. The bill in Congress that changed the name of the NICHD was sponsored by Republicans and Democrats alike, and members of both parties praised Mrs. Shriver.

"Eunice, congratulations for all that you've done for mankind," said Senator Orrin Hatch of Utah, a Republican who cosponsored the bill. "We all owe you a great debt."[16]

Representative Steny Hoyer of Maryland, a Democrat, quoted Mrs. Shriver's brother, President John F. Kennedy, who said, "Although these children have been the victims of fate, they shall not be the victims of our neglect."[17]

It was an emotional moment for me to be there and see people with different points of view and from different walks of life join together in acknowledging the value of research and the inclusion of people with disabilities. Not many things drive me to tears, but there is something about my connection with Eunice Shriver and her efforts that makes me well up with emotion. What she has done for my life means so much to me.

At that same event, Mrs. Shriver was inducted into the NICHD Hall of Honor in Bethesda, Maryland. The Hall of Honor displays plaques that "recognize individuals who have made exceptional contributions to advancing knowledge of human development and improving maternal and child health."

"In the early 1960s, Mrs. Shriver urged her brother, President John F. Kennedy, to establish an institute that would conduct research on children's health and human development," said Elias A. Zerhouni, MD, director of the NIH, in announcing the dedication of her plaque in the Hall of Honor. According to NIH,

She later worked with House and Senate leaders to help ensure passage of the legislation that would make the institute a reality. Eunice Kennedy Shriver sought to create a research endeavor that would seek to understand human development throughout the life process, focusing on developmental disorders, including intellectual disabilities, and illuminating important events that occur during pregnancy and childhood. . . . This year, as we commemorate the forty-fifth anniversary of the institute, we gratefully acknowledge the contribution of Mrs. Shriver, without whom the institute would never have been founded.[18]

After the formal ceremony, Eunice Kennedy Shriver, Senator Ted Kennedy, and their sister, Jean Kennedy Smith, stood to greet the guests attending the event in a receiving line in the Natcher Auditorium's foyer. The line was quite long, perhaps more than five hundred people who wanted to shake hands with Mrs. Shriver. I wanted to make sure to let her know how grateful I was for her pioneering and tireless efforts and how proud she had made me. I squeezed through the lines, losing touch with where my parents were. I finally was able to shake her hand.

> **Focusing on IDD**
>
> Fifteen university-based research centers make up the Eunice Kennedy Shriver Intellectual and Developmental Disabilities Research Centers Program. The children's hospitals and universities in the program are looking for ways to diagnose, prevent, and treat intellectual development disorders (IDD). The goal is to make life better for people with IDD. Mrs. Shriver was a member of the institute's first advisory council, and she helped guide the way the centers were set up. Her son, Dr. Timothy Shriver, is on the advisory council.

She had a big smile and said, "David, I will see you at our home for the reception."

That was an exciting surprise, and I asked if my parents could come, too. She said they were invited as well. I was thrilled to be part of her close circle of friends, and I felt that in some ways I was part of her extended family.

TALKING TO THE ADVISORY COUNCIL

Ten years later, I had the chance to talk to Dr. Timothy Shriver at the advisory council meeting I mentioned at the beginning of this chapter. Dr. Shriver is on the National Advisory Child Health and Human Development Council, continuing in the tradition of his influential mother. He is also chairman of the board of Special Olympics.

And now I was part of the research, too. I was proud of that, and I am glad the men and women of science are starting to see how important people with Down syndrome can be to their research. But I wanted them to know that we've just begun to explore my condition and untold discoveries await them.

"We need more research, more results, more guidance on how to improve everyone's life," I told the council.

Prenatal testing should not be about eliminating the fetus, but rather about understanding us, giving unbiased information to parents, allowing researchers to explore cures that will help us overcome limitations that slow down our development and social inclusion.

I am very fortunate in having lived a good life, but that is not the case for many others who have not had the support of family, community services, and an environment that helps them thrive, learn, and reach their full potential. I think research is needed, and the extra chromosome may unlock discoveries that benefit not only those with Down syndrome, but also the larger population. Anything that can give us an edge to lead fulfilling lives is worth pursuing.

I don't know if what I said changed anyone's mind. But the world is changing. The chairman of the advisory council, Dr. Melissa A. Parisi, gave a presentation at that same meeting about sophisticated new techniques to study people with intellectual and developmental disabilities.

I can hope. I can take part in research. I can use my skills to persuade people to support research.

What will you do?

A Small, Important Request

On the agenda, we were first cited as the "Voice of the Patient." My mother spoke with Dr. Melissa A. Parisi and requested it to be changed to the "Voice of the Participant" to better reflect my involvement with research as an individual rather than a sick person needing a cure. Dr. Parisi, in her opening remarks, thanked us for the request for the change and thought it was most appropriate and reflected better the relationship. My remarks and those of my mother were the "Voice of the Participant" next to the other scientific presentations on trends, directions, and updates from NICHD staff and their sponsored scientists.

9

THE POWER OF FAMILY
AND COMMUNITY

You're the most remarkable, because you touch people. You touch their heart, you touch their soul. You're not just tolerated, you are accepted; that has come a long way in our life together.

—John Egan, father[1]

Now you know a lot more about me. What I am today has been shaped by who I am and the people I have met in my life. Being included in everything—family life, school, sports, work—has given me chances to grow as a person that would have been hard to imagine when I was born in 1977.

I want to tell you one more story. To me, it really shows how the powerful love and pride of my family combines with the desire for people to see me as a whole person, someone who is many more things than a man with Down syndrome.

In the summer of 1985, my mom, my sister Teresa, and I traveled to the Old City of Jerusalem to visit my maternal grandmother. I was eight years old. Grandma Batato was so happy to have us in the same house where my mom grew up. Grandma—I called her Teta—was a beautiful lady, and people who see photos of her think they are of my mom. They have a lot in common; both are bright and loving.

It was hot and sunny in Jerusalem. Teta told me that I looked handsome with my big glasses and hat. She said, "You can wear it all the time, if you want."

Mom was not sure why I would not take off my cap, even inside the house.

"This is what Teta wants," I told her.

My mom asked about that and found that Teta had not told anyone in the neighborhood that I had Down syndrome. Teta had met me before on a visit to the United States, so she knew I was pretty capable. She loved me as a grandson first and accepted all of me right away. She saw I was more like all the other kids than anyone would have expected. So, while I was visiting her neighborhood, the glasses under the brim of my hat would hide my eyes, which were definitely the eyes of a boy with Down syndrome.

Teta was bright, indeed. Why have people judge me before they knew me?

"With the hat, no one will see him as a child with Down syndrome," she told my mother.

Teta wasn't ashamed of me. She was proud of me and wanted people to see me for the bright, active, inquisitive, talkative person I was. Maybe later they'd notice the little differences Down syndrome brings to the mix.

It was 1985, remember, and American society was only slowly creeping toward more acceptance and inclusion of people with intellectual disabilities. People in the Middle East held to traditional beliefs that did not lead to quick acceptance of someone with disabilities of any kind. It was that way in many countries then and still is now.

Grandma's ploy had good intentions, but it didn't go over well with my mom. She took it upon herself to let others in my grandma's neighborhood know that I had Down syndrome and that it was okay. I was a little boy like all the others, and I could swim and play ball like the other kids.

I love my family. They could have been overprotective of me, but they balanced their concerns with my need—which is everyone's need—to push my limits and learn what I can do.

I worked hard at crawling when I was tiny. I climbed into the dishwasher to help with the glasses. I raced in swimming, and I threw, hit, ran, and caught in baseball when I was young. I earned my way to jobs in competitive employment. Throughout the years, I succeeded in becoming an advocate for people with Down syndrome. My parents, John and Kathleen, worked together as a team to make life as meaningful and purposeful for me as possible. My brother, Marc, and sisters, Teresa and Miranda, just knew me as David, their older brother, as we grew up together. They kept me on my toes, and I also gave them daily lessons in accepting differences and celebrating individuality. Throughout my life, caring people showed me ways to reach for my goals. They never gave me an excuse to feel sorry for myself.

My intellectual disability has always been with me, and I've accepted it, knowing my own talents and skills truly define who I am deep down. It took lots of practice to get the hang of new ideas and ways of doing things. I have felt most comfortable with routine and predictability. But I recognized beautiful souls when I saw them. I thrived on the unexpected joys of meeting new people. And I know that I have given people in my life things of value and memories to hold tight. I am a contributor.

In this chapter, I want to give people who've changed my life a chance to talk about my impact on their lives. I asked the people whose words are in this chapter to comment on me for this book. Their views are from their responses in face-to-face, e-mail, or written communication.

MY SIBLINGS

My siblings are the ones who know me best and have spent the most time with me, and we have our own perceptions of one another. My sisters and brother see me as one of them, learning from one another and relying on one another. Here's a little about each one.

My sister Teresa is three years younger than me, but at times people would think she was the oldest in the family. I learned quite a bit from being around a sister who advanced quickly as a young child. I lagged in my development because of Down syndrome, and I wanted to catch up with her. She motivated me to excel. Teresa is talented in more than one subject, and I admired her multifaceted skills. Many would say my sister growing up was striving to be a perfectionist, while I was striving just to catch up. She truly was my role model and travel companion for the first years of my life.

"David has big dreams for himself and for all people with intellectual disabilities," Teresa wrote. "Fortunately, he's supported by a great team of people (especially our mom) who help him realize his dreams."[2]

Teresa is right. I have learned from her. But I also had the chance to teach her some things. One evening at the dinner table, Teresa was complaining about students in her class who kept asking the same questions again and again. That sounded familiar to me. I had sometimes been the person in a classroom who needed some repetition and some time to sort through complex concepts. It seemed natural to me to ask for help when I needed it.

So when she paused for a moment, I said, "Maybe they have Down syndrome like me and they need more time to understand and catch up."

Teresa didn't reply, but I could see she was thinking about what I had said.

As we grew up, Teresa shared her experiences of growing up with me in workshops for our local Down syndrome association. It's helpful for siblings to share what it's like to have a brother (or sister) with a disability. Talking about it gives everyone insights about how life and relationships in families like ours are often just like every other family. Down syndrome plays a role, of course, and it can be challenging. But it's just one feature among many features that shape how family members get along. Teresa even talked about having me as a brother at a big conference with the National Down Syndrome Congress. Siblings from throughout the United States attended with their families. It can be a relief to hear how other brothers and sisters get along with their siblings with Down syndrome. So Teresa's leadership and point of view were important to share, and I was proud of her because of that.

My sister Miranda is nine years younger than me.

Here's what she wrote:

> When I think back to my childhood memories, what stands out the most is how normal it all was. We bonded over the yardwork assignments from dad; fought over who got to control the TV remote; and how many pieces of pizza we got during TGIF night. As we both grew older, we continued to be part of each other's lives, and we would seek to include each other in small and big family and personal events.[3]

Miranda also recalled a conversation she had with our mother when she had her alone in the car after swim practice one day.

> I asked matter-of-factly, "What does Down syndrome mean?"
>
> I was in grade school and must have heard people talking about David. Mom mentioned something about an extra chromosome. She then said, "David can do everything you can do, it just takes him longer, and at times he may need more help." Her response made perfect sense to me. I always knew my brother was a little different, but at the same time, not that different at all.

Miranda got deeply involved with Special Olympics. She worked as a volunteer at Special Olympics headquarters in Washington before and after the 2007 Special Olympics World Summer Games in Shanghai. She is an experienced and effective event planner, and helped arrange a White House visit for Special Olympics athletes going to Shanghai. I wasn't going to the Games, but I went to the White House because of my connection with a Games sponsor. I am always eager to expand my network, so I made sure I handed my business card to President George W. Bush. The Secret Service agents perked up right away, wondering what I had given him. As I expected, I didn't hear back from the president. (I also didn't get to go to China, but Miranda did.)

During her senior year as a business major at Christopher Newport University, Miranda organized an Inclusion Awareness Day on campus. She coordinated with university staff, students, community organizers, and local Special Olympics offices. Best of all, she got Tim Shriver, who was then the chairman and CEO of Special Olympics International, to visit and give one of his amazing, passionate speeches.

My Miranda is also a travel buddy. I thoroughly enjoyed my trip with her to Dublin, Ireland, for the World Down Syndrome Conference in 2009. It was a celebration of the fiftieth anniversary of the discovery of trisomy 21 by Jérôme Lejeune, a French geneticist who lived and worked in Paris.

We connected with Karen Gaffney and her parents, Jim and Barbara. Karen and I have met quite often at conferences where one or both of us were speaking. Karen remembers well our Irish adventure. She commented on it as follows: "One evening, we all came back to the hotel after a day of workshops and we turned on the local news. And guess what????? There was David, all dressed up in his suit and tie that he wore to all the sessions, being interviewed by the local press! All of us from the States *loved* it!"[4]

I must say I made a bit of an impact with my appearances in the Irish news. The next day when Miranda and I grabbed a taxi, the driver said, "Eh, don't I know you from the telly?" This happened a few times that day. Miranda and I both had experiences in Dublin that touched us and we remember well. Many related to the powerful program at the Down syndrome conference. Another not nearly as moving but quite fun experience was a visit to the Guinness Storehouse, a huge brewery in Dublin. Karen and her family went along with us. We had a great time far from home. It's a great memory.

When Miranda married, she and her husband, Travis, wanted me to play an important role in the life of their first son, Mason. They chose me to be Mason's godfather.

"We wanted David to be a role model to Mason and for Mason to have exposure to individuals with differences," Miranda said. "They both have things to learn from each other, and to me that is what real inclusion is and how David makes a difference."[5]

I don't often get emotional, but when I talk about my family, especially my niece and nephew, I feel a great conviction and purpose to be a role model for them. It hits me deep down because family means so much to me, and I cherish the next generation.

My brother Marc is twelve years younger than me. I showed him how to play ball, and pretty much any sport he is good at, he is good at because of what I taught him; however, he thinks I also taught him how to "truly look at individuals as just that—individuals."

Marc wrote,

> My brother has taught me to learn from and acknowledge evident weaknesses, but to also champion and boost strengths. I take that mindset to heart. I truly see, acknowledge, and lift those around me in their strengths and weakness, from colleagues to close friends. My brother David has defined and shaped my life beyond any one person. The impact of his being who he is and what he teaches me cannot be overstated. It's the skill I rely on most to make my way through life, and I think I do a pretty good job thanks to him.[6]

Marc is my Special Olympics coach for Unified Softball and Unified Soccer. All the athletes love and respect him. He is very dedicated to and caring toward each of the athletes. I recommended him for his first summer job as an intern on Capitol Hill with Congresswoman Cathy McMorris Rodgers when he was a sophomore at Virginia Tech. (I had met with her soon after her son Cole was born with Down syndrome. We established a strong connection and a lasting friendship.) Right now, Marc is my partner in speaking engagements at high schools and community occasions. We also volunteer together at Special Olympics events. We have run into the frigid Atlantic Ocean for the Polar Plunge in Virginia Beach. We traveled together to the 2011 Special Olympics World Summer Games in Athens, Greece. We drove to New York City for World Down Syndrome Day at the United Nations in 2012. And he and I are a team as research participants in projects funded by the National Institutes of Health (NIH).

Things were not always easy between my younger brother and me. Marc and I remember a time when he was first able to drive at sixteen years old. We got into a fierce argument in the car. I had the feeling he was telling me what to do, and as a grown man, I really resented that. I resented it so much, in fact, that I just got out and walked home. And a long walk home it was. It gave me a lot of time to think. For me to come to grips with that fact that my little brother might know best sometimes was a hard reality; however, my brother always treated me with respect as the eldest and didn't belittle me. Our respect for one another and acceptance of one another's skills formed the toughest of bonds between us from then onward. We are close allies.

MY BROTHER'S FRIENDS

I value how much my brother has included me in his life and circle of friends. Jared Gold, Marc's friend and the web developer for my site, explained how it works:

> I've enjoyed the privilege of being David's friend for about fifteen years now. David is the only person with Down syndrome I've ever really gotten to know (so far). We've shared many memories, laughs, victories from pickup sports games, and even some beers. Being David's friend over the years has been rewarding not just for friendship's sake, but, moreover, in learning about how to interact with others, which includes correcting my own misconceptions and shortcomings when it comes to engaging with those that I might consider different from me. David has joined myself and the rest of Marc's friends for many an adventure. David brings his sense of humor and the tenacious smart-alecky wit that we've all come to appreciate. He adds not an element of his apparent Down syndrome, but an impact because of his one-of-a-kind personality. He has become integrated into the dynamic of our circle. We intentionally treat David like everyone else in the group, which often includes some good-natured ribbing, a hallmark of the Egan family. Having David as a friend has been enjoyable, enriching, and rewarding. I'm one of the lucky few who have had the opportunity—which means I feel responsible to help inform others that they should not miss out on such an experience.[7]

When my parents are away on travel and it coincides with my birthday, my siblings always make sure to have a celebration for me. Marc and his friends gave me an awesome surprise birthday party a few years ago in downtown Washington, DC. I have fond memories of spending time with them.

Kallan Krocker, another of Marc's friends, joined me at a car-racing event with Special Olympics. Ram Khalsa, a former roommate of Marc's, would listen to me practice my speeches and give me feedback. Patrick Hunt, an acclaimed videographer, and Mike Engle, another close friend of Marc's, took the time to help film me as part of my application to be a Special Olympics Sargent Shriver International Global Messenger and create a video for my birthday. Just like Jared, they have followed me closely throughout the years and supported me.

JULINE KALEYIAS, MY SISTER-IN-LAW

I met my future sister-in-law, Juline Kaleyias, when my brother invited her to our house to watch an episode of *Game of Thrones*. I was the first family member to meet her. We sat in the cool, dim basement. I talked about Marc's previous girlfriends, which Juline found interesting. But we also talked about my siblings and brothers-in-law.

Said Juline,

> David proudly and energetically described the Egan sibling gang. . . . I instantly picked up how tight-knit they were, and if I was ever going to marry Marc that I would be marrying into the family, which I eventually did. After spending these past three years with David, I've observed that he initiates more conversation about his family than politics, international affairs, Special Olympics, and any other topic he is passionate about. He is very proud to be the eldest brother, and I am happy for David because I sense he has inner peace and is comfortable in his shoes as the head of the siblings.

Juline follows my journey of advocacy, attending speeches and going to events with me. She also plays on our Special Olympics Unified Softball team. She's our star shortstop, and everyone loves having her on the field. She's a full member of my family and a big contributor.

She wrote,

> The Egan family's team effort has shaped David into the man he has become. The support system they provided David has been phenomenal. One of the first times I spent quality time with David's mother, Kathleen, we were in the garden of the Franciscan Monastery in Washington, DC. There she described each of her four children at length and how they differed from one another.
>
> Everyone's unique involvement has led to David's happiness, success, and ability to inspire others. His sister Teresa and his father John's overachiever personalities pushed David beyond his limits starting at a very young age; this gave David confidence each time he improved at something new.
>
> Miranda and Marc, the gregarious of the family, often organize family activities that bring everyone together, which gives David a sense of belonging. And Kathleen—Kathleen has been with David every step of the way, nurturing David and providing him with that maternal, selfless love. Confidence, belonging, and love are all qualities that every human being deserves. I enjoy being around David, especially when we joke around. It inspires me when I hear him speak in front of a crowd and

observe people's reactions to him. David grounds me, and his presence reminds me how to put life into perspective. I'm lucky to have met David, and I'm glad that we can be part of each other's lives.[8]

TERESA'S HUSBAND, MATT PHILIPP

When Matt married my beautiful sister Teresa, I was one of the grooms-men in the wedding. Matt is more than just my brother-in-law. He is my friend, my movie and sports TV buddy. We enjoyed many outings, a few beers, and some laughter before they moved from Virginia to California. Every time they visit, we sneak in a good movie.

Matt remembers when Teresa invited him to meet the family.

"The moment I met David at his home, he immediately ushered me into his bedroom to show me his wall of fame, covered with his numerous awards and medals earned over a lifetime of sporting competition. The pressure was on," Matt wrote.

I remember telling Matt to watch out and be nice to my sister because I was her big brother, and I cared about her.

Matt is fun and easy to talk to. So we often sat in the kitchen chatting over a snack. That is where we were when he said something that shocked me. I had just finished telling a story, and he said, "Oh man, that's retarded."

Matt wrote the following about that incident:

David's eyes grew wide as his jaw dropped; to his credit he didn't make me feel as stupid as I now know those words made me sound. Instead of belittling me, he casually invited me over to his computer and Googled the Special Olympics PSA for the "R" Word Campaign. That twenty-nine-second video quickly eliminated my gaping social blind spot, bringing my stupidity into crystal clear focus.

It's so obvious now that words do carry meaning and have the power to uplift or suppress; I was lucky enough to have David as my teacher for these life lessons. To this day I sincerely appreciate David's forgive-ness of my stupidity, and I used that same video in my own classroom over the next decade any time one of my students mindlessly described anything using the "R" word. It doesn't matter whether or not I in-tended to be mean, the reality was that I was being mean to my new friend right to his face.

It's hard to imagine that in 2004, a song titled, "Let's Get Retarded" was the first single to ever sell over a half-million digital downloads, sweeping the band Black Eyed Peas into American pop cultural con-science. Thankfully, the Black Eyed Peas eventually decided to remix their hit song, changing the title and lyrics to the much more inclusive "Let's Get It Started," instead of the original "Let's Get Retarded." That new song earned them a Grammy Award for Best Rap Performance by a Duo or Group in 2005. Four years later, after my gaffe, I thoroughly enjoyed going crazy on the dance floor with David to that new and improved song at my wedding to his sister!

Looking back, I now realize that it is not possible to foster a truly inclusive environment if I myself continued to use any words that stigmatized, isolated, and excluded others. In fact, the biggest gift that David has imparted on my life is his perspective of what true inclusion looks and feels like in real life. According to David's teachings, true inclusion seems to be a combination of treating him the same as I would anybody without intellectual and developmental disabilities while keeping in mind that he might require an accommodation to level the playing field. I was lucky enough to marry his lovely sister Teresa two years after erasing the "R" word from my vocabulary.[9]

MIRANDA'S HUSBAND, TRAVIS FULK

Travis is my brother-in law, but he is also my friend, my next-door neighbor, and the father of my nephew, Mason, and niece, Mira. He is also my weekly companion to exercise at a nearby recreation center and grab a bite after the workout, and maybe a beer for good measure. He is a true friend. I enjoy spending the one-on-one time with him at the gym and afterward.

When I asked Travis for input, he wrote,

Many years before meeting David, I had a friend and next-door neighbor with Down syndrome. When the opportunity came to meet David for the first time, I felt as though I had a good idea of what to expect. Imagine my surprise. David asked me numerous questions that night and at one point even asked me what I thought of U.S. foreign policy. I was not prepared. Looking back, I'm sure David was sizing me up. After all, I was dating his younger sister, Miranda, and I could tell the protective big brother was keeping a watchful eye on me. David still finds ways to catch me off guard, and even in seemingly innocuous conversation he often finds a way to challenge my ideas, whether intended or not.

Miranda and I got married, and in the fall of 2012, we bought the house across the street from David's. Previously we had been a three-hour drive away, and now we were a thirty-second walk away. Since I was living extremely nearby, David saw his opportunity. He challenged me to get involved in Special Olympics with him. I was hesitant at first. I wasn't sure if I'd have the time or if I would even have anything to contribute, but before I knew it, I was helping with Special Olympics softball and soccer. Needless to say, it's been an amazing experience, and without David's challenge I likely would have missed out on it.

David and I have a weekly workout routine that involves weightlifting followed by lap swimming. It's a great opportunity for us both to spend some time together and improve our shapes while we're at it. We typically go on Wednesday nights and grab dinner afterwards, so it also ends up being a nice way to break up the week. David's an excellent swimmer, which is apparent as soon as he hits the water—and in the number of medals hanging on his bedroom wall. I grew up on the Eastern Shore of Virginia, surrounded by water, and always counted myself a strong swimmer; then I swam with David. Our first time in the pool, I think David swam about four times farther than I even could. David was obviously a competitor, and I was more of a survivalist. David still takes time to try to teach me different strokes and how to do flip turn. I try to teach him proper form on the bench press. I guess you could say we're both works in progress.[10]

FRIENDS IN ADVOCACY

I've made many friends in the disability community, and one of my favorites is Nancy Mercer. She is well known and highly respected in our community. For more than thirty years she has been a champion for the needs of people with intellectual and developmental disabilities throughout their lifespan. She believes in inclusion.

I met Nancy when she was the executive director of the Arc of Northern Virginia, and Jill Egle was her coexecutive director. I met Jill first, and she told Nancy she should meet me. They drove together to my home in Vienna and came to the front door.

Nancy wrote,

> We were met by a handsome young man with warm eyes and a welcoming, "Hello." We had the opportunity to meet David's mother and his father, quickly learning that the "apple does not fall far from the tree" when it came to "passion when talking about the disability movement." David's mother, Kathleen, shared the family's vision for ensuring David had every opportunity his brothers and sisters would have from the day he arrived—and how this "vision" has become David's passion as a man living with ID/DD.
>
> It was one of those "memorable moments" that one does not forget, as I sat in the sun with Jill and David—two powerful self-advocates, sharing their wisdom, life stories, and time with me. I quickly could

see why Jill thought David was so special; in addition to having a quick smile, twinkle in his eye, and being quite charming—he was incredibly smart and passionate about the disability movement. David was someone I wanted to get behind and support!

Since that afternoon in May, I have had the great fortune of being included in David's life as he takes risks and opens doors for himself and others with ID/DD to follow. When David was picked to be the first man with an intellectual disability to be a Joseph. P. Kennedy Jr. Public Policy Fellow on Capitol Hill, I knew life as we knew it would never be the same.

Through Special Olympics, as a Global Messenger, I watch David travel the world, speaking to groups—large and small—about the importance of building communities for people with ID/DD. David's message translates into all languages, as it is one that speaks to "Honoring the human value of all individuals—through words, actions, and deeds."

I have seen David serve on multiple boards of directors; provide direction to the business community on how to hire and retain employees with ID/DD; continue to "Spread the Word to End the Use of the 'R' Word"; and become a proud uncle as his siblings build families of their own.

I have known David Egan for over a decade and have been in awe as I have watched him change the world—once again, Jill was right, "David has what it takes to make the world a better place—for all of us!" I am glad he is my friend.[11]

A DIFFERENT KIND OF INCLUSION

I am going to take a big step back and tell you about a kind of inclusion that has meant a lot to my family and me. When I was born, my parents were graduate students working on doctorate degrees at the University of Wisconsin–Madison. They had a group of friends at the time who have stayed in touch throughout the years. Several of their friends were from Mexico. In addition to being graduate students in genetics, business, chemical engineering, food services, and medicine, they were talented musicians.

Sometimes when a baby is born with a disability, friends don't rally around. Remember, at that time, having a baby with Down syndrome was considered a tragedy. It would have been easy for my mom and dad's friends to fade away and become distant. Instead, they bonded together ever tighter. Those bonds are just as strong today, and the group has expanded into what we call the Wisconsin Clan. That support was important to my parents. And throughout the years, it became important to me, too.

The group came together because of a couple named Bill and Harriette Rosenbaum. They lived near Madison and were a host family to several foreign students. The Rosenbaums held parties for the students they hosted and their friends. I was too little to remember it, but I know that Eduardo and Andres played guitar, and Edmundo played the violin. Bill Rosenbaum did magic tricks and made a balloon crown for my little head. We had potluck dinners and smashed pinatas. I had rhythm in my blood, and dancing came natural to me.

Now, every two years, we have a reunion. Different families host in their home cities. The biggest reunion was in Washington, DC, when my family was the host. It was 2007, and we had fifty people at that memorable gathering. Our tradition was to have a welcome party at a place that represented the culture and history of the host's town. My parents booked a reception room on Capitol Hill. We had representatives from the Mexican Embassy there, plus Representative Rubén Eloy Hinojosa of Texas joined us.

I had the honor of being the welcoming speaker, and I said,

> Buenas noches, amigos. . . . You have known my family for over thirty years. Several of you honored my parents by playing at their wedding, and most of you were graduate students at the University of Wisconsin. They told me about all the parties, singing, dancing, soccer games, volleyball, and holiday celebrations. We all keep great memories.

I thanked Harriette Rosenbaum for making it all possible all those years ago. Then I went on:

> I saw pictures of me with Uncle Eddy playing the guitar, sleeping in Rich's arms, playing ball with Edmundo and Andres, hitting a pinata with Carlos, and enjoying the fun with many others. That was about thirty years ago when I was a kid, and I think it is because of people like you that we understand the meaning of friendship, family, and sharing. It is because of people like you that our world is a better place and I am able to lead a normal life and be successful.

The reunion lasted three days. We took a river tour of the city and played soccer near our home in Virginia. The connection with the group has stayed strong. My parents invited some of the group to my thirty-fifth birthday party, and they did not hesitate in making a special trip to celebrate with me. The musicians played "Las Mananitas," the Mexican happy birthday song. I felt very grateful to have such good friends near and far who care about me.

IN MY COMMUNITY

I live in Vienna, Virginia, a beautiful little town in the metropolitan Washington, DC, area. It was named one of the top places to live in the United States. The people in Vienna are friendly. I love the small-town feeling, with lots of trees, bicycle paths, town greens, and beautiful homes. The town has great community services and is only a few miles from the cultural treasure in DC. Mountains and beaches are both less than one hundred miles away. We live on a quiet cul-de-sac well away from traffic and near a pretty park. The area is full of big shade trees. It was a good place to grow up and a wonderful place for me to live.

> **Our Home**
>
> We have been living in the same house for more than thirty years. Every now and then, my parents would think of moving. I always reminded them that my bus stop is next door and the Metro train station is within walking distance. Those discussions ended, and they decided to remodel our home to make it roomy and comfortable for a family of six.
>
> I love where we live and do not have a desire to move or live by myself. I feel independent and self-sufficient, while at the same time I have the support of those who love me. When my family travels, I enjoy having the entire house to myself now that my brother and sisters are married and have their own places.

I know many of my neighbors, and I think many more know me. My family and I take part in activities at our church. I feel very connected to my community. I know my way around, I know many people, and I know how things work. I would like to share some of the comments people sent me about having me in their community.

Brendan and Biljana McKinley, our backyard neighbors, wrote about getting to know our family at a winter holiday party in 2009:

> I remember hearing from David about his story of growing up in Vienna, his journey as an athlete, his efforts for advocacy, and his professional accolades. It was hard to not be humbled by his accomplishments, and we had fun looking at some unbelievable photo albums documenting his global journey.
>
> David told us about his 20-year career at Booz Allen Hamilton. It was truly refreshing to hear his story of overcoming challenges and persevering over such a long period of time, especially while so many Americans choose to switch jobs every year or two. Hearing about his

career and broader journey to get where he is today is something that we will never forget.

One of the many blessings David has given the world is positively impacting those privileged enough to be part of his life. We count ourselves among these folks and have shared David's story with our family, friends, and colleagues. His message has inspired us, and we could not be prouder to be his neighbors![12]

Shirley Nunn shared her impressions of me as a church member at St. Mark's Catholic Church in Oakton, Virginia, where I worship. One of her weekly challenges is making sure that everyone who needs to be in place for worship services is there. I'm a willing volunteer as an altar server, one of three people who serve that role at every service. I was included in religious education and well prepared to be junior and senior altar server. She liked that I would check in before services to see if she needed help. She often did, and I was happy to do it.

"Cheerfulness and reliability: To be sure, David has been my all-time favorite senior altar server at the parish," she wrote. She also wrote that I was a mentor for those around me.

Among the most well-regarded roles that anyone can assume in society is that of mentor. When asked to explain it, I've said that a mentor is a person who sees something of themselves in you. Furthermore, that person is willing to give direction and supply ideas for growth and achievement that you may not have considered at all. The mentor finds ways to open doors to further connections for the one under their wing. David Egan fills that role.

Let me emphasize the word *willing*. It's a quality at the heart of paid and pro bono employment alike. In my view, giving beyond what others expect makes the world go around. I've seen up close David's willingness to assist.

Year round, I hear and read about his achievements. . . . David is in the mentoring business. An uncountable number of people with developmental disabilities are being recognized directly because of his voice and energy. He is advancing the next generation of mentors.[13]

During the last few years, one of my closest friends has been David Thomason. He is vice president of advancement at Special Olympics Virginia. We began working together through the Athlete Leadership program at Special Olympics. We've traveled throughout Virginia and the United States, and even the world, together. I've learned so much from David's calm and patient approach to challenges. And it turns out, he wrote that he has learned from me, too.

"David is an influencer. His words are powerful, but his example even more so," David wrote in an e-mail to me.

> How he lives and leads his life speaks volumes. I've witnessed it many times, and I welcome the opportunity to see it many more. It happens in those times when David fervently puts the eloquently crafted words of his speeches into action, as he so often does, resulting in that moment when—because of spending time with David and getting to know who he is (and, as importantly, who he is not)—a person's mind is changed, their perspective is shifted, their choices affected. It's a gift that we all want and one that comes so naturally to David.[14]

I've grown to be a leader and live a life of inclusion. My family and extended family—neighbors, teachers, friends, mentors, coaches, and employers—all played roles in my growth and accomplishments. In their own way, each helped me build confidence, independence, and pride. In my own way, I opened their eyes to the fact that people with disabilities, especially people with Down syndrome, are the sum of many characteristics.

In my life, I have learned that the barriers of low expectations aren't real. In a way, they mark the limits of imagination. If someone hasn't seen or heard of someone doing something, maybe they think it can't be done. The solution, as I see it, is to do that thing and grow the understanding of what people with Down syndrome can do. As Science Officer Spock would say, it's logical that if one person with Down syndrome can do something that people thought was impossible, it wasn't Down syndrome that placed the limit.

As my life unfolded, I wanted to live the idea of "boldly going where no other person with Down syndrome has gone," to borrow from *Star Trek* once more. I let myself dream big and then bigger. I dared to dream of work that mattered. I dared to dream of advocating for an entire world of people with Down syndrome and other disabilities. I dreamed of being on Capitol Hill, saying the words that changed hearts, minds, and laws.

By daring to dream, I found many of my goals turning into accomplishments. I didn't do any of it alone. Who does? That's what inclusion is, isn't it? Being part of a community of people who share ideas and responsibilities and lives.

Let's go!

Boldly.

ACKNOWLEDGMENTS

Throughout my life, I've been blessed with a growing community of supporters. As I lived and grew to be an adult, my family, friends, coworkers, and supporters helped me achieve things I'm proud of. They were all proud, too. Many people, especially my godmother, Alice Erickson, began to ask me, "When are you writing a book about your extraordinary life?"

Alice, my dear godmother, I have the answer to your question: The time for me to tell my story is now. Thank you for encouraging me and urging me to share what I have learned. You were confident that I could do it, and that helped me believe it, too. You are one of the biggest supporters in my worldwide community of people who want the best for me and help me achieve it.

This is the story of my life, written by me, but it's not the first time I've been featured in a book. I was surprised when Paul Eder, Raoul Davis, and Kathy Palokoff included me in their book *Firestarters: How Innovators, Instigators, and Initiators Can Inspire You to Ignite Your Own Life*. Paul Eder found me on my website, took a chance on me with an interview, and ended up giving me one of the biggest opportunities and platforms of my life. From that book to workshops, Paul and I have made a great team. Raoul Davis promoted my message in the public with our creation of DavidEganSpeaks on Facebook. Kathy Palokoff helped with the original memoir proposal you are reading and got us started on a path for success. Thank you, Paul, Raoul, and Kathy. You are the reason I've written this book. You opened a new path and taught me how to grab the attention of the book-publishing market. Thanks to Leticia Gomez of Savvy Literary Services, who tirelessly worked with all of us to find the perfect publisher.

I also learned that writing a book is a project that can only be done right with a community of supporters and contributors. I want to thank all of you who responded to my call for support when I shared that I wanted to write a memoir. My supporters are broad and diverse. I am so thankful to each one of you for sending stories, quotes, and comments to enrich my own content. You reminded me of things I may have forgotten. You gave me your own perspectives, leading me to see things in new ways.

I am humbled and so appreciative of the insightful and encouraging way that many of you described me. Some sent a paragraph, and some sent pages. Even if your contribution is not literally included in the book, it is not because it did not make me smile or I did not like it. Many found their place in this book, while I am saving others for future writings on my social media and website, at davideganadvocacy.com.

For all of the written stories, events, and quote contributions, I sincerely thank Sujata Bardhan, Nicki Pombier Berger, Erin Croyle, Mary Davis, Karen Gaffney, Jared Gold, Barbara Haight, Rita Holstein, Rick Jeffrey, Shane Kanady, Dave Lenox, the McKinley family, Nancy Mercer, Shirley Nunn, Joe O'Brien, Sylvia Piper, Parker Ramsdell, Vincent Randazzo, Lisa Roti and family, David Thomason, Michelle Witten, Roy Zeidman, and Rachelle Zola.

An unexpectedly helpful contribution came from our friend Kate McKenna, who connected my mom and me to Will Schermerhorn, our partner in writing and editing this book. Will is a longtime friend, but we did not know that he had more skills than just photography, videography, and online content marketing. Kate told us about his power of the pen and ability to transform our written words into powerfully structured chapters with key memories and messages. We learned quickly that more did not mean better. I enjoyed our face-to-face meetings and his passion to partner with us in this writing journey.

I want to send a sincere thank you to everyone else who has had a role in my life. You are too many to mention here, but you will recognize yourself in my stories. I am thankful to my employers, my community, and the many organizations, especially Special Olympics, the Down syndrome community, and the Arc, which I serve and interact with, and which supports people with disabilities. You play a crucial role in advocating and opening new paths for all of us. A shout out also to all those who, like me, have an extra twenty-first chromosome and other disabilities. We all rock, and my story mirrors many of your stories. The future is bright, and I am filled with gratitude.

Throughout my life, my family has been the bedrock of my support, and I am indebted to each one of you. Thank you for your support, as well as your eagerness and interest, in seeing my project succeed. To my sisters, Teresa and Miranda, thank you for sharing your views of what it means to live with a brother who has Down syndrome. To my brothers-in-law, Matthew Philipp and Travis Fulk, thank you for sharing your perspectives. To my sister-in-law, Juline Kaleyias, thank you for revealing our family's inner circle traits and reviewing many chapters with a keen eye for detail and clarifications. To my brother Marc, thank you for sharing your stories and reading every single chapter, helping to rewrite and expand content in ways that truly made a difference.

Last but not least, I want to acknowledge my parents. They inspire me every day and are always ready to make my path brighter. I want to thank my dad for telling the stories and believing in me. Without my mom, this book would not have been started and completed. She gave it every free hour she had and worked diligently to ensure that we are telling a compelling story that will inspire people both with and without disabilities to believe in themselves and pursue their dreams. Thank you, Mom. You are my number-one champion.

NOTES

INTRODUCTION

1. Quote from Vincent Randazzo, public policy advisor to the National Down Syndrome Society (NDSS) and certified leadership coach at Capitol Knowledge, LLC, in an e-mail, July 7, 2019.

2. "Facts about the Connection between Down Syndrome and Alzheimer's Disease," *Global Down Syndrome Foundation*, https://www.globaldownsyndrome.org /about-down-syndrome/facts-about-down-syndrome/facts-about-the-connection -between-down-syndrome-and-alzheimers-disease/ (accessed January 3, 2020).

CHAPTER 1

1. Quote from Erin Croyle, writer/journalist/advocate and Partners in Policy-making alum, in an e-mail, September 1, 2019.

2. "World-Renowned U of U Medical Geneticist John M. Opitz, MD, to Receive 2011 William Allan Award in Human Genetics for Pioneering Work Identifying, Understanding, Genetic Syndromes," *University of Utah Health*, October 7, 2011, https://healthcare.utah.edu/publicaffairs/news/archive/2011/10-07-11 _John%20Opitz%20Award.php (accessed July 11, 2019).

3. "World-Renowned U of U Medical Geneticist John M. Opitz, MD, to Receive 2011 William Allan Award in Human Genetics for Pioneering Work Identifying, Understanding, Genetic Syndromes."

4. Rick Herber, Elmer W. Ramthun, and Patricia Brown, *Waisman Center Interactions* (Madison, WI: Information Services, April 1980), WECP booklet.

CHAPTER 2

1. Quote from Nicki Pombier Berger, oral historian, in an e-mail, August 2019.

2. "About IDEA," *Department of Education*, https://sites.ed.gov/idea/about-idea/ (accessed July 11, 2019).

3. Seville Allen, "Education and Civil Rights," *Future Reflections* (Winter/Spring 1991), https://actionfund.org/images/nfb/Publications/fr/fr10/Issue1/f100113.html (accessed July 11, 2019).

4. "John F. Kennedy and People with Intellectual Disabilities," *John F. Kennedy Presidential Library and Museum*, https://www.jfklibrary.org/learn/about-jfk/jfk-in-history/john-f-kennedy-and-people-with-intellectual-disabilities (accessed July 11, 2019).

5. "John F. Kennedy and People with Intellectual Disabilities."

6. "John F. Kennedy and People with Intellectual Disabilities."

7. This quote and the following quotes and information are from Rachelle Zola, in e-mails, June 13, 2019 and June 17, 2019.

8. Zola, e-mails, June 13, 2019 and June 17, 2019.

9. Zola, e-mails, June 13, 2019 and June 17, 2019.

10. Zola, e-mails, June 13, 2019 and June 17, 2019.

11. Rachelle Zola, *Simple Successes: From Obstacles to Solutions with Special Needs Children* (Denver, CO: Outskirts Press, 2006).

12. Zola, *Simple Successes*, 3.

13. "WWRC Admissions," *Wilson Workforce and Rehabilitation Center*, https://www.wwrc.net/Admissions.htm (accessed July 11, 2019).

14. Pamela Fayerman, "All Children Do Well at Some Things and Not Others: Son's Ability 'Amazes' Mom," *Vancouver Sun*, August 24, 2006, A1, A10.

15. Quote from Karen Gaffney, in an e-mail, July 31, 2019.

16. Quote from Nicki Pombier Berger, in an e-mail, September 3, 2019.

CHAPTER 3

1. Quote from Travis Fulk, in an e-mail, August 2019.

2. Story by Rick Jeffrey, president of Special Olympics Virginia, in an e-mail, July 2019.

3. Quote from Parker Ramsdell, in an e-mail, June 2003.

4. Quote from Marc Egan, in an e-mail, August 2019.

5. Quote from Dr. Sujata Bardhan, in an e-mail, August 6, 2019.

CHAPTER 4

1. Quote from Mary Davis, CEO of Special Olympics, Inc., in an e-mail, August 29, 2019.

2. Paul Eder, Raoul Davis, and Kathy Palokoff, *Firestarters: How Innovators, Instigators, and Initiators Can Inspire You to Ignite Your Own Life* (Amherst, NY: Prometheus, 2018).

3. Eder, Davis, and Palokoff, *Firestarters*, 185–88.

4. Nicole Trifone, "Lighthearted Style Proves Successful for New Coach," *Patch*, January 25, 2012, https://patch.com/virginia/oakton/lighthearted-style-proves -successful-for-new-coach (accessed July 11, 2019).

5. David J. Egan, "Dare to Dream, Special Olympics," *Spirit Magazine* 5, no. 4 (2000): 27.

6. Quote from Dave Lenox, president and CEO, Special Olympics Washington, in an e-mail, September 3, 2019.

7. Lenox, e-mail, September 3, 2019.

8. "Paul Berry," *HistoryMakers*, https://www.thehistorymakers.org/biography /paul-berry (accessed July 11, 2019).

9. Quote from Dave Lennox, in a letter, October 2000.

10. Quote from Lisa and Todd Roti, in an e-mail, July 2019.

11. "Achieving a Better Life Experience Accounts (ABLE), 2019 Edition," *Social Security Administration*, https://www.ssa.gov/ssi/spotlights/spot-able.html (accessed July 11, 2019).

12. Quote and information from David Thomason, vice president of advancement, Special Olympics Virginia, in an e-mail, July 2019.

13. Thomason, e-mail, July 2019.

CHAPTER 5

1. Quote from Sylvia Piper, CEO of Disability Rights Iowa, in an e-mail, June 13, 2019.

2. "Why We Matter: Mission," *Best Buddies*, https://www.bestbuddies.org/what -we-do/mission-vision-goals/ (accessed July 11, 2019).

3. "Improving Employment Opportunities for People with Intellectual Disabilities," *U.S. Senate Committee on Health, Education, Labor, and Pensions*, March 2, 2011, https://www.help.senate.gov/hearings/improving-employment-opportunities -for-people-with-intellectual-disabilities (accessed July 11, 2019).

4. "Improving Employment Opportunities for People with Intellectual Disabilities." Subsequent quotes are from the HELP Senate hearing.

CHAPTER 6

1. Quote from Ralph Shrader, in an e-mail contribution to the DSANV Employment pamphlet, December 2008.
2. Quote from Barbara Haight, in an e-mail, May 2019.
3. Haight, e-mail, May 2019.
4. National Down Syndrome Society, "Launch: Careers for People with Down Syndrome," YouTube, 2015, https://www.youtube.com/watch?v=o7g6bhyOP6k (accessed July 11, 2019).
5. "Easter Seals Honors Elizabeth Dole and Dr. Ralph Shrader," May 15, 2015, https://washingtonexec.com (accessed July 11, 2019).
6. Quote from Joe O'Brien, senior vice president, CBRE/Advisory and Transaction Services, in an e-mail, September 18, 2019.
7. "Why SourceAmerica?" *SourceAmerica*, https://www.sourceamerica.org/about (accessed July 11, 2019).
8. "David Egan: Employment Advocate," *SourceAmerica*, https://www.source america.org/special-olympics (accessed July 11, 2019). https://www.sourceamerica .org/stories/david-egan-employee-advocate
9. Quote from Shane Kanady, vice president, SourceAmerica Workforce and Business Development, in an e-mail, July 2019.

CHAPTER 7

1. Quote from David Thomason, in an e-mail, Summer 2019.
2. https://nihrecord.nih.gov/newsletters/2008/03_21_2008/story1.htm (accessed June 18, 2019).
3. Richard Sandomir, "The Mother of Special Olympics," *New York Times*, August 12, 2009, https://www.nytimes.com/2009/08/12/sports/12sandomir.html ?searchResultPosition=1 (accessed June 18, 2019).
4. "Kennedy Foundation Selects 2010 Fellows: Two AUCD Network Members Selected," *Association of University Centers on Disabilities*, July 13, 2010, https://www.aucd.org/template/news.cfm?news_id=5512&parent=964&parent _title=View%20All%20News&url=/template/page.cfm?id%3D964 (accessed June 18, 2019).
5. "Children's National Karen Summar Receives Prestigious Joseph P. Kennedy Foundation Public Policy Fellowship," August 9, 2011, *Children's National*, https:// childrensnational.org/news-and-events/childrens-newsroom/2011/childrens -national-karen-summar-receives-prestigious-joseph-p-kennedy-foundation-pub lic-policy-fellowship (accessed June 18, 2019).
6. Official letter from Ralph W. Shrader, PhD, chairman and CEO, Booz Allen Hamilton, October 28, 2014.
7. Official letter from Karen L. Summar, MD, MS, October 27, 2014.

8. Official letter from Cathy McMorris Rodgers, member of Congress, October 28, 2014.

9. Joseph P. Kennedy Jr. Public Policy Fellowship application by David Egan, October 2014.

10. Official letter from Steve Eidelman, executive director, Joseph P. Kennedy Jr. Foundation, January 27, 2015.

11. "Our Mission," *National Down Syndrome Society*, https://www.ndss.org/our-story/mission/ (accessed June 18, 2019).

12. "DSWORKS Employment Program," *National Down Syndrome Society*, https://www.ndss.org/work/dsworks/ (accessed June 18, 2019).

13. "Resources for Employers," *National Down Syndrome Society*, https://www.ndss.org/resources/resources-for-employers/ (accessed June 18, 2019).

14. "Valued, Able, and Willing to Work: Employing Individuals with Down Syndrome," *National Down Syndrome Society*, http://www.ndss.org/wp-content/uploads/2017/10/Valued-Able-and-Ready-to-Work-3-9-16.pdf (accessed June 18, 2019).

15. Quote from Roy Zeidman, in an e-mail, June 28, 2019.

16. Bill Plaschke, "Special Olympics Opening Ceremony Is Out of This World," *Los Angeles Times*, July 31, 2015, https://www.latimes.com/sports/olympics/la-sp-special-olympics-plaschke-20150726-column.html (accessed June 18, 2019).

17. Quote from Shane Kanady, in an e-mail, August 26, 2019.

CHAPTER 8

1. Quote from Michelle Whitten, cofounder and executive director, Global Down Syndrome Foundation, in an e-mail, November 8, 2019.

2. Speech at NIH, January 18, 2018.

3. Waisman Center, https://www.waisman.wisc.edu/.

4. Quote from Rita Holstein, in an e-mail, July 2019.

5. Holstein, e-mail, July 2019.

6. "Ventricular Septal Defect," *American Heart Association*, https://www.heart.org/en/health-topics/congenital-heart-defects/about-congenital-heart-defects/ventricular-septal-defect-vsd (accessed July 11, 2019).

7. Erna E. Ziegel and Mecca S. Cranley, *Obstetrics Nursing*, 8th ed. (New York: Macmillan, 1984).

8. Ziegel and Cranley, *Obstetrics Nursing*, 228.

9. "Parallels in Time: A History of Developmental Disabilities," *Minnesota Governor's Department of Administration Council on Developmental Disabilities*, https://mn.gov/mnddc/parallels/five/5f/1.html (accessed July 11, 2019).

10. "Mission Statement and Guiding Principles," *University Center for Excellence in Developmental Disabilities*, https://ucedd.waisman.wisc.edu/mission-statement-guiding-principles/ (accessed July 11, 2019).

11. Elizabeth Hecht to Kathleen Egan, invitation flyer sent in an e-mail, July 3, 2013.

12. "Anita Bhattacharyya," *University of Wisconsin–Madison*, https://crb.wisc .edu/staff/bhattacharyya-anita/ (accessed July 11, 2019).

13. https://niad-project.org/details.html

14. M. Degerman-Gunnarsson et al., "Pittsburgh Compound-B and Alzheimer's Disease Biomarkers in CSF, Plasma, and Urine: An Exploratory Study," *Dementia and Geriatric Cognitive Disorders* 29, no. 3 (2010): 204–12, doi: 10.1159 /000281832. https://www.ncbi.nlm.nih.gov/pubmed/20332638

15. "201901 INCLUDE Project Clinical Trial," *National Institute of Child Health and Human Development*, https://www.nichd.nih.gov/about/advisory /council/archive/201901/INCLUDE-project-clinicaltrial-IDDB-201901 (accessed July 11, 2019).

16. https://nihrecord.nih.gov/newsletters/2008/03_21_2008/story1.html (accessed July 11, 2019).

17. Ibid.

18. "NICHD Renamed for Eunice Kennedy Shriver, Advocate for Institute's Founding," *National Institutes of Health*, March 3, 2008, https://www.nih.gov /news-events/news-releases/nichd-renamed-eunice-kennedy-shriver-advocate -institutes-founding (accessed July 11, 2019).

CHAPTER 9

1. "What's Up with Down Syndrome," *Attitude*, May 14, 2017, https://attitude live.com/watch/What-s-Up-With-Down-Syndrome-The-future (accessed August 28, 2019).

2. Quote from Teresa Egan Philipp, in an e-mail, September 2019.

3. Quote and the following quotes from Miranda Egan Fulk, in an e-mail, August 2019.

4. Quote from Karen Gaffney, in an e-mail, July 2019.

5. Egan Fulk, e-mail, August 2019.

6. Quote from Marc Egan, in an e-mail, August 2019.

7. Quote from Jared Gold, in an e-mail, August 12, 2019.

8. Quote from Juline Kaleyias, in an e-mail, September 7, 2019.

9. Quote from Matthew Philipp, in an e-mail, June 2019.

10. Quote from Travis Fulk, in an e-mail, August 2019.

11. Quote from Nancy Mercer, LCSW, founder of Inclusion Consultants, in an e-mail, May 2019.

12. Quote from my neighbors, the McKinley family, July 2019.

13. Quote from Shirley Nunn, in an e-mail, July 2019.

14. Quote from David Thomason, in an e-mail, July 2019.